PATCHWORK

— AND —

QUILTING

A STEP-BY-STEP GUIDE

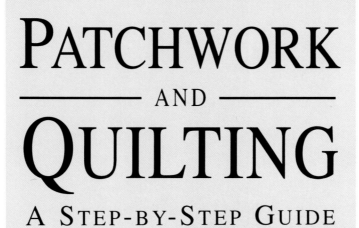

PATCHWORK

— AND —

QUILTING

A STEP-BY-STEP GUIDE

GAIL LAWTHER & ANGELA BESLEY

CASSELL

First published in the UK
1994 by Cassell
Villiers House
41/47 Strand
London
WC2N 5IE

British Library Cataloguing-in-Publication Data
A catalogue record for this book is available from the
British Library
ISBN 0 304 34480 X

This book was designed and produced by
Quarto Publishing plc
The Old Brewery
6 Blundell Street
London N7 9BH

Senior Editor: *Honor Head*
Editor: *Maggi McCormick*
Senior art editor: *Amanda Bakhtiar*
Designer: *Sheila Volpe*
Illustrator: *Sally Launder*
Photographers: *Paul Forrester, Chas Wilder*
Picture Researcher: *Carmen Jones*
Picture Manager: *Rebecca Horsewood*
Art director: *Moira Clinch*
Publishing director: *Janet Slingsby*

Printed in Singapore by Star Standard Industries Pte. Ltd

CONTENTS

INTRODUCTION

Quilting is easy and quilting is fun! If you're a beginner, we encourage you to explore the pleasures of quilting. Use this comprehensive book to take some of the mystique out of this ancient, beautiful and very satisfying craft by learning the basic cutting and stitching techniques for all kinds of different quilts. If you're already an accomplished quilter, you'll find this book a useful reference for your library. Experiment with new techniques and use the projects and the examples of fine historical quilts shown on the following pages for inspiration.

The history of quilting is long and varied. *Patchwork and Quilting* begins with the Story of Quilts, an introduction to different types of quilts. It includes a visual overview of historical examples, ranging from a spectacular appliquéd Baltimore album quilt to modern Seminole patchwork.

The second section, Quilting Basics, discusses the materials and equipment that you will need to make the projects in the book. It also teaches all the fundamental skills, such as estimating material required, making templates, marking and cutting fabrics, piecing by hand and machine, joining blocks and adding borders, assembling a quilt top, quilting by hand and machine and finishing the quilt edges. These are techniques you will need for making the sampler quilt in the next section and they will help you stitch many more patchwork and quilting designs, traditional and modern.

The next section, the Sampler Quilt, takes you step-by-step through the stages of making a quilt, from creating nine different blocks to the final binding. Every stage is clearly shown, so that you learn how to make the various blocks, add sashing, make and add a chess-board border and finally mark, quilt and finish your quilt. If you do the lessons in this section, you will end up with a beautiful sampler quilt in traditional colours.

Extending Your Skills introduces some of the more unusual types of piecing and quilting, including Sashiko, trapunto, Italian, wholecloth quilting and English patchwork. Each new skill features full instructions for a simple project.

The Pattern Library illustrates a wide range of the most popular quilting and piecing designs. Use these for your own projects or substitute them for some of the designs used in the sampler quilt.

The final section gives you advice on restoring, caring for and displaying quilts. A glossary of common patchwork and quilting terms is in the back of the book.

1

The story of quilts

The story of patchwork and quilting is extensive and intriguing. Techniques are rooted in the practical details of everyday life in times before most people had the leisure to pursue arts and crafts for their own sake. Piecing was a necessary skill, so that leftover dressmaking scraps or the best parts of worn clothing could be used and re-used for economy when fabric was still a precious commodity. People kept

HISTORY

The story of quilts

warm with quilting on clothes and bedcovers; soldiers wore quilted armour and padded jackets for protection.

But human beings are naturally creative and as patchwork and quilting developed, different designs began to appear. Rather than piece or stitch haphazardly, sewers began to use particular patterns, which were refined and developed while being handed down from generation to generation. Craftspeople, itinerant workers and patternmakers spread new ideas to different areas; certain places and peoples developed their own specialized techniques, a process which continues today.

To give you an overview of some of the main types of quilting, we have put together a gallery of fine historical examples, showing the skill and versatility of our ancestors.

Shells, flowers and interlocking chains have been combined in this wholecloth quilt dating from 1935; the main motifs have been set off by the contrasting chessboard background texture, worked both straight and diagonally.

WHOLECLOTH QUILTING

Wholecloth quilts are not pieced, but are made from a background fabric and decorated with stitched patterns. Wholecloth quilting dates back several hundred years in many traditions, especially in the North of England, Wales and North America. The fabrics and waddings used depended on the materials most easily available in the area. The quilting is often worked in the same colour thread as the background fabric, although occasionally a contrast colour is used. The traditional quilting stitch is a running stitch, worked through all three layers of top fabric, wadding and backing fabric; the stitch holds the wadding in place.

The designs of wholecloth quilts were usually inspired by everyday objects – leaves, flowers, feathers, goose tails and wings, cords, fans, shells. Leaf shapes were often created by drawing using a flat-iron as a template; one side of the iron would be traced, then turned around for the other half of the leaf shape. Because quilting was usually done in groups, it is difficult to know where the traditional designs originated; individual quilters would add their own touches to the chosen patterns.

AMERICAN BLOCK QUILTS

Traditional American quilts were often pieced in square blocks. Stitching one block made the work easily portable and blocks could be stockpiled until there were enough for a whole quilt top. In the earliest quilts from colonial days, the seams were stitched by hand. With the advent of the sewing machine, the stitching became much quicker, but many quilts are still pieced by hand in blocks.

The range of block designs is phenomenal, many of them with evocative names like Oh Susannah, Goose in the Pond, Rising Star, and Steps to the Altar.

It was customary for an unmarried girl to piece quilt tops and store them in her Hope Chest. When she became engaged, her friends and relatives would join in, add remaining layers of wadding and backing, then stretch, stitch and finish the quilts, helping her get ready for her new life as a married woman.

Despite the wandering appearance of the overall pattern, this quilt is actually made in blocks; pieced blocks of 25 squares alternate with plain white blocks that have had small squares appliquéd in the corners. The design is known as Irish Chain.

AMISH QUILTS

The Amish people take their name from Joseph Amman, a Swiss who was a model of conservatism. When William Penn invited persecuted people to join him in his new land, the Amish went from Switzerland, Germany and the Alsace to America. Still clinging tenaciously to their clothing styles, traditions and religious observances from centuries past, the Amish people today live apart from their fellow countrymen and follow a simple way of life.

With this stress on simplicity, it is easy to appreciate the stark beauty of the Amish quilts.

Many of them are made from the plain hand-dyed fabrics also used in the traditional Amish clothing. Sometimes large sections of plain, coloured cloth are used in the quilts instead of pieced blocks.

The quilts may have one or more borders and are always quilted with exquisite and intricate designs, sometimes stitched in a contrasting colour such as orange or purple. Often the large areas of pure colours are offset by black borders or binding, adding to their overall striking appearance.

The vivid colours, multiple borders and central diamond of this quilt are all typical features of Amish quilts – finished with exquisite quilting in every section.

15

ENGLISH PATCHWORK

English patchwork differs dramatically in technique from American patchwork but possesses an equally noble history. The earliest known example dates from 1708. In English patchwork, the fabric pieces are tacked over paper shapes, then sewn together to form a simple or complex pattern. As with many other techniques, English patchwork from different eras varies in appearance with the kind of fabrics that were fashionable at the time. When exotic prints were imported in large quantities from the Middle East in the 19th century, patchwork was made from those; later on Britain began producing inexpensive cotton print fabrics and the appearance of the patchwork changed accordingly.

During Queen Victoria's long reign, patchwork made from pieces of plain, coloured silk became extremely popular; certain patterns, such as diamonds and hexagons, were especially in vogue. English patchwork has been very useful for social historians because it was often worked in scrap fabrics such as pattern samples from mills. Also, the papers used in the inner templates were often cut from old letters, ledgers and books and provide fascinating information when pieced together from unfinished bits of patchwork.

The bright colours, unpatterned fabrics and geometric design of this quilt, dating from the end of last century, are typical of English patchwork.

The red dye used on this quilt, dating from the turn of the century, was known as turkey red and was one of the most popular colours for this kind of simple appliqué.

APPLIQUÉ

Appliqué has been around for many centuries. From Ancient Egypt to the present day, appliqué has been used to mend and decorate clothes and furnishings. Traditional appliqué in quilts involved arranging fabric shapes – often natural forms such as petals, leaves, berries, animals or feathers – in a pleasing design on a background. The fabric shapes were then sewn into place with tiny invisible stitches; raw edges were turned under so they didn't fray or were held in place with a decorative stitch.

Early appliqué quilts often used a simple colour scheme, perhaps one or two strong colours on a plain white background. Some of these quilts were called turkey quilts because a certain shade of red, known as Turkey Red, was a popular choice. Another form of applied stitching was crazy quilting – random shapes of patchwork, often made from velvets and other fancy fabrics, were embellished with embroidery, beadwork, and patriotic slogans. Broderie persé was also popular; this method involved cutting motifs from several printed fabrics, arranging and stitching them onto a background fabric, and embellishing the new design if desired.

A spectacular example of a Baltimore album quilt, featuring many complex and beautifully executed appliqué designs, including many typical garlands and vases of flowers and several versions of the American eagle.

ALBUM QUILTS

Album, or friendship, quilts are a specialized type of quilt originating in America. The original album quilts were usually done as gifts, perhaps for a wedding or if a friend was moving. These quilts are generally stitched in blocks, but in true album quilts, each block is a different design and often was stitched by a different person. Christmas Cactus and Basket blocks were favourite designs, and occasionally three-dimensional flower motifs were appliquéd; the designs are sometimes breathtakingly detailed. The colours and patterns were usually carefully chosen so that the whole quilt harmonized when assembled; red and green on a white background was a favourite colour scheme. On some examples the names

SEMINOLE PATCHWORK

The Seminole Indians of Florida developed very distinctive patchwork designs in strip-pieced patterned bands. The technique seems to have developed in the late 1800s when the sewing machine became available to them.

The technique involves strip piecing two or more long pieces of fabric and then cutting the new fabric into secondary strips. The secondary strips are then laid out and joined in a new relationship to each other, forming patterned bands which can be quite complex.

The Seminole Indians generally use the bands on garments rather than quilts, but they can be used to create large decorative pieces as well.

Many different geometric patterns can be seen in this striking example of Seminole patchwork, worked in a limited colour scheme of bright plain fabrics set off by the black border.

or signatures of the quilt makers were embroidered on the blocks.

The most spectacular examples of album quilts were done in the Baltimore area, so album quilts are often known as Baltimore quilts. Genuine Baltimore quilts are highly sought after. Album quilts are still made today; they are popular as community projects.

The spiky plant design of this Hawaiian quilt, worked in plain fabrics appliquéd on to a white background, is typical Kapa Lau work.

HAWAIIAN APPLIQUÉ

Hawaii has developed its own form of appliqué called Kapa Lau. It is made by stitching one large, carefully shaped piece of fabric onto a plain background. American missionaries showed the islanders how to fold paper and cut it into shapes like simple plants or snowflakes; the unfolded paper was then used as a pattern for cutting the appliqué fabric. Hawaiians soon developed their own designs and the original small patterns became larger and larger, many of them based on the luxuriant foliage of the island such as pineapples, breadfruit trees, ferns, palms and paw-paws.

Once the design has been cut out, it is tacked to a background fabric and the edges are carefully turned under and stitched down. This is a very time-consuming process, for some of the designs are extremely complicated. Once the appliqué is complete, the area beyond the appliqué is usually quilted with echo quilting – lines of stitching that echo the outline of the appliqué shape.

20

TRAPUNTO QUILTING

Trapunto, or stuffed, quilting is a specialized technique that involves stitching two layers of fabric together in shaped pockets which can then be stuffed. Stuffing is inserted through the backing fabric (if it is loosely woven) or through a slit which is later sewn closed. Raised appliqué work of this kind is common in ecclesiastical embroidery.

In 18th- and 19th-century trapunto quilts, most of the quilt would be quilted in the ordinary way, then a central motif or medallion was given an extra layer of stuffing to raise it. It is an effective way to draw attention to a particular part of a design.

This quilt shows an attractive combination of appliqué and quilting in a subtle colour scheme; the border of grapes and the delicate outer border provide an attractive frame for the central design.

ITALIAN QUILTING

Italian, or corded, quilting involves threading cords through channels stitched in a double layer of fabric; the corded design stands out in relief from its background. Despite its name, it did not develop solely in Italy; corded quilting is found in artefacts from many Asian and Middle Eastern countries as well as European ones. Wonderful examples have survived from the 18th and 19th centuries in England of whole bedcovers decorated with tiny, elaborate, intricate corded quilting designs.

Linear designs lend themselves well to Italian quilting, but the design can be as fine or as bold as you wish. Modern quilters have experimented using everything from thin yarn to rope for the cording and leather to net for the fabric.

This corded and quilted hat dates from the early 20th century; it was made in Northern India and is stitched using techniques which date back generations.

2

Quilting basics

Making a traditional quilt is not an activity that can be rushed; that is part of its charm. There are several different stages, from choosing the fabric and working out the design, through cutting, piecing, backing and quilting, to the final finishing by binding the raw edges. The main stages of quilt making have a logical order, and in the pages that follow we take you through them one by one. Occasionally, a stage

Elements of a quilt

may not be necessary; for instance, you will not need to draw a design and make templates if you are using bought templates, but generally each step will be covered in some way.

But first you'll need to understand the terms that quilters use; like every other art and craft, quilting has its own special vocabulary. Words and phrases like tacking, wadding, piecing, sashing, setting blocks and quilt top can all seem strange and bewildering if you're a beginner, but you'll quickly become used to them, and like the stages in quilt making, they are all perfectly logical. On these pages, we introduce you to the common terms for the different parts of a quilt and the various processes involved. The same terms will be used throughout this section of the book.

Piecing or patchwork refers to pieces of fabric cut in specific shapes and then stitched together in a decorative design.

A block is a section of patchwork stitched in a regular shape, usually a square. Traditional quilts are often built up from several individual blocks; the blocks may be identical or may vary in design. In our sampler quilt, we use nine different square block designs.

Binding is the edging of the quilt, and covers all the raw edges neatly. It also contributes to the overall effect of the design. There are several ways of binding quilt edges (see page 98).

Tacking is used to hold the three layers of the quilt together; the lines of tacking threads, worked in a grid across the quilt (see page 52), hold the layers in place while they are being quilted.

Backing fabric gives a neat finish to the back of the quilt; the wadding is concealed between it and the quilt top.

A **frame** is used to stretch the fabric while it is being quilted. Frames may be large, so that the whole quilt can be stretched at once, or small enough for one section to be quilted at a time (see page 54).

Quilting *refers to the stitching which passes through all three layers of the quilt (top, wadding, and backing); the quilting provides both texture and decoration. Quilting may be done by hand or machine (see page 96).*

A **border** *is a decorative edging of plain fabric or pieced work added around the main quilt area. Borders can be made from one or several fabrics, plain or patterned (see page 150). This is a plain border with a quilted design.*

Sashing *or* **setting strips** *refers to strips of fabric used to separate blocks in a quilt. In some quilt designs, blocks are joined without any sashing so that new patterns are formed (see page 38).*

Wadding *is used to pad the quilt, and provides texture and bulk. Various kinds of wadding are available to suit different requirements (see page 52).*

25

W hile there is plenty of specialized equipment available to help the quilter, not
very much of it is essential; most of the tasks of
making templates, cutting and piecing fabric,
and marking and stitching quilting patterns
can be done with general drawing and sewing
equipment that you will probably already have
in your house. If you are just beginning
quilting, start off with the essentials, marked

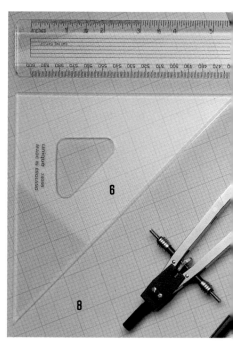

Equipment

with a bullet (•) below; they will provide all
that you need to make the projects in this
book. As you want to extend your quilting
skills, acquire the more specialist items listed:
they will save you time as you cut and stitch.

▶ **General sewing equipment**

- **1** *Large scissors for cutting fabric*
- **2** *Small, sharp-pointed embroidery scissors*
- **3** *Selection of sewing needles*
- **4** *Quilting needles*
- **5** *Thimbles*
- **6** *Safety pins*
- **7** *Tape measure*
- **8** *Cotton or polyester sewing thread*
- **9** *Tacking thread*
- **10** *Quilting thread*
- **11** *Pins, preferably glass-headed (they are easily visible and can't*

accidentally be ironed over)
- **12** *Extra-fine pins for silks and satins*
- **13** *Flat-headed pins (useful when machine-stitching as they don't catch in the foot)*
- **14** *Beeswax and beeswax holder*

Even-feed foot for sewing machine
Sewing machine
Thumble (used on the thumb of your quilting hand)

◄ **General drawing equipment**
- **1** Pencils – both medium-hard and soft, HB and 2B
- **2** Pencil sharpener
- **3** Eraser
- **4** Short and long rulers (30 cm/12 in and 60 cm/24 in)
- **5** Crayons or felt-tip pens
  - **6** Set square
  - **7** Protractor
  - **8** Graph paper
  - **9** Set of compasses

▼ ► **Frames**
- Quilting frames (you will only need one type: circular, rectangular, oval, roller, slate, floor-standing, full-size)

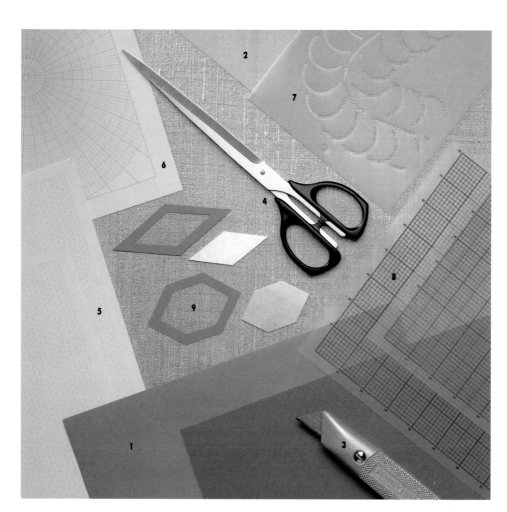

◄ Templates and template materials

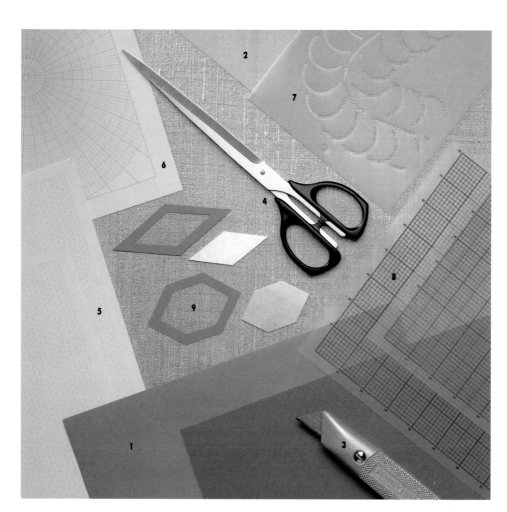

◄ Templates and template materials

- **1** *Card*
- **2** *Plain template plastic*
- **3** *Scalpel*
- **4** *Paper scissors*
- **5** *Isometric graph paper*
- **6** *Polar coordinate graph paper*
- **7** *Quilting templates in different designs*
- **8** *Sheets of template plastic marked with guide rules*
- **9** *Window template (for positioning a printed motif accurately within the template shape)*

Patchwork templates in different designs

► Equipment for cutting accurate fabric patches

- **1** *Rotary cutter*
- **2** *'Self-healing' specialized cutting mat with cutting guides for templates*
- **3** *Sandpaper grips (used on the corners of rulers and templates to stop fabric from slipping while you cut)*
- **4** *45° Kaleidoscope wedge ruler*
- **5** *Omnigrid (a useful guide for cutting many different templates)*
- **6** *Multi Miter (a guide for mitres of different angles)*
- **7** *Scrapsaver ruler*
- **8** *BiRangle for cutting half rectangles*
- **9** *Magic Star for cutting 8-pointed stars*
- **10** *Quilter's Rule*
- **11** *9 in Wedge Ruler*

Large rotary cutter
Quilt and Sew ruler
Easy Angle (for cutting accurate triangles)
Lip edge ruler
Pineapple ruler (measures accurate 45° sections)
Salem ruler (a guide marked with 60° and 45° angles)
Super Seamer ruler (for adding seam allowances to templates and fabric pieces)

◀ **Equipment for marking fabrics**

• **1** *Soluble-ink pens (marks can be removed with cold water)*

2 *Fading-ink pen (marks fade gradually when exposed to air)*

3 *Coloured pencils*

4 *Cloth markers*

5 *Transfer pencil (for drawing iron-on transfers)*

6 *Tracing wheel with chalk holder*

7 *Prick and pounce wheel*

8 *Dressmaker's carbon paper (available in several colours)*

9 *Blunt tapestry needles*

10 *Fabric eraser (for removing ordinary pencil marks from fabric)*

11 *Quilter's quarter (adds 5 mm/¹/₄ in to straight edges)*
Bodkin
Silverpoint (pencil-shaped metal implement used for marking fabrics)

In the early days of patchwork, people would simply use what was available, usually the best parts left in worn-out clothing or bedding. In fact, that was how the whole craft of patchwork began; it was born from necessity, when fabric was expensive and thrift was the order of the day. Nowadays, most of us buy patchwork fabrics new for each project, and there is an endless variety to select from: wool, cotton,

Choosing fabrics

◀ **Cotton**
All of these fabrics are 100% cotton in different thicknesses. Cottons come in myriad patterns and plain colours, and are the ideal quilting fabrics. Glazed cotton and chintz have a shiny finish which looks very pretty in plain quilted areas; the finish is diminished, though, by hot washing, and it makes it more difficult to work the quilting.

synthetics and novelty fabrics such as lamé, fur, plastic and leather. In addition, many of these fabrics are available in a multitude of colours, patterns and textures, which can make your choice bewildering. How do you decide whether to use plain or printed fabrics? Large or small prints? Should you mix different types of fabric?

Although it seems a very mundane consideration, the first thing to decide is whether the finished article will need to be washed. Obviously, if you are making a quilt for your bed, a pillowcase, or a garment, at some stage the item will need washing, so you will have to use a fully washable fabric. The most suitable is lightweight 100% cotton, which holds its shape well, is washable and is easy to stitch through several layers if you are quilting. Polycottons are available in many pretty plain colours and printed patterns, but generally they aren't so satisfactory for quilting; they slip around more while you are working on them, can be rather translucent and are often more difficult to quilt through several layers.

All the fabrics you plan to use in a washable item must be soaked in warm water to pre-shrink them and to test them for colour fastness. Light- to medium-coloured ones can be washed by machine on a warm cycle, but dark colours are more likely to run and should be washed separately. Rinse the fabric until the water runs clear; if colour is still bleeding from it after about six rinses, discard it – it could

◀ **Polycotton blends**
These fabrics are attractive, but don't have the density or firmness of cotton.

◀ **Polyester fabric**
Many polyester fabrics are unsuitable for quilting because they are slippery and loosely woven, but others, such as the firm polyester silks shown here, can be used to great effect in patchwork and quilting.

◀ **Satin**
Satin has a wonderful sheen and can be very dramatic used in stained glass patchwork (see page 108).

ruin many hours of work if it bleeds when your finished patchwork item is washed. Once the fabric is dry, check whether the grain is straight; the visible horizontal and vertical threads (warp and weft) should be at right angles. If they aren't, gently pull the fabric diagonally to straighten the grain. Then press the fabric to remove the creases caused by washing. If you wash and press your fabrics as soon as you buy them, when inspiration strikes, you're all ready to cut and sew!

Some types of silks and satins can be washed; others have to be dry-cleaned; check with the supplier when you buy them, and don't mix the two types. Generally it's better to use the same kind of fabrics in a patchwork item – for instance, all cottons or all silks – unless you are mixing them for a particular effect. If you want the look of silk without the expense and the washing difficulties, polyester silks are available.

Finally, if you're making something which won't be washed, you can use any fabric. Thick fabrics such as linen, sailcloth and twill are usually too thick to be pieced or quilted successfully, while wool fabrics such as Vyella are often too thin and too loosely woven. However, there are plenty of other fabrics to experiment with. Lamé patches here and there on a jacket or wallhanging give a wonderful sparkle; nets and voiles can be layered over other fabrics to create new tones and depths of colour; fur fabric and leather could make realistic animals on a child's wall quilt. Exotic silks, satins and velvets make a rich setting for the embroidery on a crazy quilt.

◄ Silk
Silk is available in many different weights, weaves, colours and textures. The firmer weaves are very satisfactory for patchwork; the finer ones can be very slippery. Some silks are woven to produce novel effects, such as heavy slubs; 'shot' silk has different colours for the warp and weft threads and shimmers between the two shades.

◄ Net and voile
These fabrics aren't firm enough to use for patchwork on their own, but they produce interesting special effects in experimental work.

◄ Metallic fabric
Metallic fabrics are generally wholly or partly synthetic, and come in a dazzling variety of finishes. They can be used with conventional patchwork patterns to make exotic items such as evening jackets and glittery bags, but have the drawbacks of other synthetic fabrics. Also, they have a very strong visual impact, so don't overdo them.

GRAIN LINES

Good fabric should have the long grain running parallel to the selvedge (the finished edge). Check this before buying, because if the grain is not true your pieces may become distorted. Templates should always be placed straight along the grain. In a woven fabric such as cotton, the long grain is sometimes known as the warp, while the yarn woven across this at a 90° angle is the weft.

Once you've decided on a patchwork pattern, the next important decision is colour. You may want to match or contrast with something in your decor or an outfit, and this may determine the dominant colour for your patchwork. Or, you may want the patchwork to have a certain 'feel', for instance, a vibrant look or a soft gentle effect. Patchwork patterns themselves often suggest to the quilter the kind of colour

Choosing colours

schemes that would suit them. However, it is possible that you don't have any ideas about colour and are starting from scratch; in this case, you can have great fun working out your colour scheme.

Certain colours go together naturally, especially when they have a similar underlying colour. For instance, blues that tend towards green rather than purple move towards yellow in the colour wheel; green-blues tend to look harmonious with yellows and creams. In the same way, purple-blues go well with pinks because they both move towards red in the colour wheel. Other colours create a vibrant reaction and set each other off in different ways; this is especially true of the complemen-

◄ Shades of one colour
Although we divide the colour wheel into six basic colours – red, orange, yellow, green, blue and purple – each individual colour can have an almost infinite number of tones or variations in hue. The fabrics here are all green, but you can see the enormous variety of shades, from acid lime-green to a dark olive green.

◄ Light and dark
All colours range from dark – very dark in some cases – to pale. The lightness or darkness of a colour is known as its 'value'. Aim to have fabrics of several different values in your block; otherwise it may look bland and lack contrast.

Even a simple colour wheel like this can help you to understand how colours relate to one another. Colours close together, such as the blues and purples, harmonize because they are the same 'family'. The colours shown far right are the complementaries, which are opposite one another on the colour wheel. These set up strong contrasts, so use them sparingly unless you want a particularly vibrant, dramatic effect.

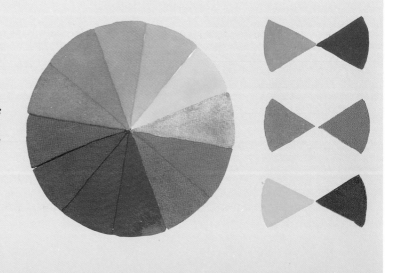

tary colours, which are directly opposite each other on the colour wheel – green and red, purple and yellow, orange and blue. Colours which are quite close to each other in the colour wheel can create dramatic clashes – for example, red and puce, purple and turquoise, blue and lime-green.

If you're starting your colour scheme from scratch, visit a fabric shop or department store with a wide choice of cotton fabrics and pick two or three which please your eye when they are put together. Stand back to check the overall effect. If one is 'killed' by the others, discard it and choose another. Continue until you are completely satisfied with your selection.

◄ **Vibrant colours**
Red and green, the strongest pair of complementary colours, create strong contrasts which can be effective on a small scale. You can play down the contrast by varying the proportions of the colours or by introducing some neutrals.

◄ **Clashing colours**
Some colours set up a discordant effect which can be dramatic. The lime green and dark turquoise are not natural partners, but such colours can be used successfully if separated by another colour such as peachy-orange.

◄ **Harmonious colours**
Here, pink and mauve-pink is combined with a gentle slate grey. The effect is harmonious, with all the fabrics blending well with each other. Colours like these would give a gentle 'country' feel to a bed quilt.

◄ **Adding neutrals**
Neutral colours are those which don't appear as pure colour mixes in the colour wheel: black, white, cream, brown, beige, dark grey, muddy green etc. All neutral colours can be used to great effect in patchwork, especially in backgrounds and to set off other colours.

Small prints look good alternated with solid blocks and create a homely feel.

Some fabrics, such as gingham and damask, have patterns woven into them, but this process tends to alter the characteristics of the fabric, especially the texture. Generally, when you want to use a mixture of plain and patterned fabrics in patchwork, fabrics which have patterns printed on them are best. The patterns may be small or large, seemingly random or printed in a very regular design; some

Patterns and plains

patterned fabrics have individual motifs which can be picked out and placed in specific arrangements in your work.

Patchwork patterns can look very bold worked entirely in plain fabrics, but adding a print or two will often give an extra lift to the design and keep it from looking stark. It is possible to use more than one print in your patchwork; in fact, you can piece it entirely from patterned fabrics if you choose them carefully. The main rule of thumb is not to choose strong patterns that fight visually with each other or which obliterate the lines of the piecing itself.

Striped fabrics can be very striking and lend themselves to special effects, but avoid striped designs which are not printed along the straight grain of the fabric – they can deceive the eye into believing that the patches are cut crookedly. If the pattern isn't straight, cut with it rather than with the fabric grain.

▲ Small prints
Small all-over prints are particularly suitable for patchwork; they provide texture without distracting the eye.

Large blocks of solid colour create impact and have an immediate effect.

◄ Large prints

Large all-over prints can be very effective if used carefully, but if you use several large patterns together, you may lose the lines of the patchwork shapes themselves.

◄ Striped fabrics

Striped fabrics can have simple or complex patterns, ranging from a straightforward two-colour stripe to a multicoloured design in a random colour sequence.

USING INDIVIDUAL MOTIFS OR AREAS

You may want to use just one part of a printed fabric – perhaps a particular motif or section of a design. In this case, you will need a transparent template, so that you can be sure that you have positioned it exactly where you want it on the fabric. This technique is rather wasteful of fabric, but it does allow you to produce some very dramatic effects.

Buying fabrics for a quilt can be a costly business, so you want to be sure that you've chosen fabrics that will work well together before you invest in large amounts of them. Colouring in a sample block will give you a good idea whether your chosen colour scheme works well, but once you have a basic idea in mind, you need to start working with real fabrics. One of the best ways is to lay out a

Working it out

Making a shape come forward
When you want to emphasize a particular motif or part of a design, work the motif in the lighter fabric and set it on a dark background.

sample block using scraps of fabric cut to shape. If you have a good collection of fabrics, you may have enough to try this out without buying anything; if not, most shops will sell short lengths or small patches of fabric. Move the shapes around until you have a good balance of colour and intensity. If one fabric doesn't seem right, replace it with another one until you are satisfied with the result.

You may need to buy one fabric to blend in with several others you already have; if so, making a colour fan may be useful. Glue long thin strips of your existing fabrics on thin card, making sure that you don't leave a border of card around the fabric – this way, you can lay your fabric right up against fabrics on the bolt and see how they look side by side. Secure all the strips together in one corner with a safety pin or punch holes and put a ring through them; then you will be able to fan them out as necessary so you can see different combinations of fabric together.

Here you can see how some of the ideas in this section work in practice. All of the nine-patch blocks shown here have been made in the same design – the Churn Dash – and the same size. You can see, though, that each block looks different to the others because of the fabrics that we have chosen and the ways in which the fabrics have been arranged.

▼ *This colour fan has been made with strips of fabric glued to card; the strips have then been hooked together in one corner. The strips can be fanned out in different combinations so that they can be laid against new fabrics in the shop to assess their effect together.*

Individual motifs
This floral pattern has been carefully cut so that a flower appears in the centre of each triangle and in the centre of the middle patch. Use a clear template when you want to position motifs accurately in this way.

Making a shape recede
A dark shape placed on a light background seems to move away from you. Use this effect to reduce the emphasis of a very dramatic fabric.

Fabrics too close in tone
Although the patterns on these two fabrics are quite different, they are so close in tone that they merge together, losing the lines of the block design.

Well-balanced shades
This block has a similar background fabric as the previous one, but stronger fabrics have been chosen for the other patches so that the lines of the block design can be seen clearly.

Asymmetrical arrangements
In this block, the tones fade from light to dark diagonally. This can look very dramatic if you join several blocks made in the same way, so that the shading alters in a regular pattern.

Bright and bold fabrics
This block uses bright, acid plains and bold, brightly coloured prints, giving a very modern look to the block. The asymmetrical arrangement of the fabrics adds to the jazzy effect.

Exotic fabrics
Although cotton is the traditional choice for patchwork, you can use many other fabrics. This block has been made in subtle shades of silk, hand-dyed to give a soft and delicate appearance.

MAKING TRIAL GRIDS

If you draw your patchwork pattern (see page 40, Drawing designs) and photocopy it several times, you can use these grids to try out different colour schemes and arrangements. Use coloured pencils or felt-tip pens, depending on the intensity of colour that you want in your finished patchwork.

When you are planning your quilt, you need to decide how the different elements will go together. If you are using several blocks, will they look best joined directly to one another or separated? For the edges of the quilt, do you want a decorative border or will you simply bind the edges?

When blocks are joined side by side, they can produce intriguing secondary designs (see

Putting it together

Sashing can be used in many ways to create different visual effects. The quilt above uses sashing at angles with a half-fan motif to give a feel and look of shells or scales. The quilt right uses sashing across the block motifs to create 'quarter' blocks which are then echoed in the border.

opposite and page 146). You may decide, though, that you want each block to be seen on its own and the best way of doing this is by adding sashing, or setting, strips. Sashing is particularly important if you have made blocks in several different designs or techniques, such as for our sampler quilt; blocks in very different patterns rarely look good joined directly without sashing. Sashing should be made from a fabric that will show off the more decorative blocks to their best advantage; you might want to choose a neutral colour or one of the plain fabrics from your patchwork. Sashing can be in a patterned fabric, but since it is intended as a frame for the stronger patterns, it is best to use a small all-over print that doesn't distract the eye too much from the blocks.

Borders go around the whole quilt top and add extra visual interest; they are also a good way of increasing the size, for instance, if you want to extend a double-bed size to fit a king-size bed. A pieced quilt really calls for a pieced border, which will look most effective if it uses elements from the quilt itself – stars or diamonds for star quilts, borders with curved elements for Drunkard's Patch or Grandmother's Fan designs, squares and triangles for quilt designs made up from these basic shapes. Use the same fabrics as you used for piecing the blocks; plan the design on graph paper and work the corners out carefully so that they carry the design around well.

Here, a Churn Dash quilt has been designed with the blocks joining directly and edged with a narrow plain border.

This border for a quilt made from Card Trick blocks uses smaller versions of the shapes in the blocks.

This pieced border for the same Churn Dash design uses one third of the basic block in reversed colours, with a corner made from a square divided into two triangles. The whole quilt top is then edged with a narrow border.

In this variation, sashing one third of the width of the block has been added between the blocks and around the edges. Because of the extra width produced by the sashing, a new element has been added to the patchwork border, repeating the rectangular shapes.

These examples show two variations of a pieced border known as Twisted Ribbon.

These pieced borders look very attractive around simple pieced quilts. Here they border Shoo Fly and Jack-in-the-Box blocks.

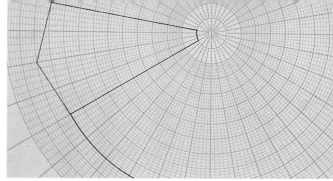

M any patchwork quilts are constructed from square blocks which are then joined, with or without separating strips of fabric (sashing or setting strips – see page 38), to make the quilt top. Other designs are based on equilateral triangles or circles divided into different segments or other arrangements of shapes. Whatever basic design you choose, it is important to know how to draw accurate

Drawing designs

▲ *For patterns using segments of a circle, draw your design on to polar coordinate graph paper at the correct size, dividing the circle into the number of segments that you need. Mark the pieces you need for templates in the same way. If the graph paper is too small for a full pattern, use it to draw the correct angles in the centre of the circle and simply extend the petal shapes out as far as needed.*

patterns at the right size so that you can calculate how much fabric you need and make perfect templates from your drawings. Once you have learned the basic principles, it is then very easy to change the size of a pattern or to change the design by altering a line or two.

Good-quality graph paper is essential for drafting patterns. It is available from stationery shops and art suppliers, and from quilting supply outlets, in both imperial and metric measurements. A transparent plastic ruler is a great help, along with soft-to-medium pencils, a good pencil sharpener and an eraser.

Graph paper makes it unnecessary to measure many of the angles, such as the angles of the triangles in a nine-patch design, but you will find polar coordinate graph paper or a compass and protractor (see page 27) useful for patterns such as Dresden Plate, which are formed from segments of a circle. Isometric graph paper (see page 26) is divided into equilateral triangles and is useful for patterns based on 60° angles and their multiples.

Once you have a full-size pattern, use it to cut pattern pieces for templates or photocopy it and colour in different versions to try out different colour schemes and examine the effect of several blocks joined side by side.

ENLARGING AND REDUCING

When you are working with irregular patterns such as appliqué shapes, you may want to enlarge or reduce them. To do this, draw a grid of squares across the original. Draw another grid containing the same number of squares, but making them larger or smaller depending on whether you want to enlarge or reduce. Now copy the main lines of the shape on to your grid; the squares will help you to see where the lines go.

1 *Choose your pattern and decide on the size of the block that you need. Your chosen size will depend on the kind of block you have chosen (see above), the number of blocks you need in your project and the size of your finished project. For this example, we will use a 30 cm (12 in) block and draw the Ohio Star design.*

▲ *For patterns using 60° angles and their multiples, draw your design on isometric graph paper at the correct size and mark the pieces you need for templates in the same way.*

2 *Draw a 30 cm (12 in) square on graph paper and divide it into 9 equal squares, each measuring 10×10 cm (4×4 in).*

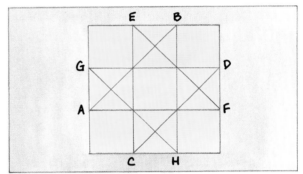

3 *Draw in the diagonals. In this example, they run from A-B, C-D, E-F and G-H. Draw each of the diagonals in one line for accuracy, even when they go across several squares.*

4 *Now work out how many individual template pieces you will need. If you look carefully at this block, you will see that although it is pieced from 21 different pieces of fabric, only 2 shapes are used – the 7.5 cm (3 in) square, and the right-angled triangle which makes up a quarter of it.*

5 *Use a scalpel to cut out one example of each piece needed. If you don't want to spoil your full-size drawing, make careful copies of the pieces needed on a separate piece of graph paper and cut them out. You now have accurate guides which you can use for making templates.*

Commercial templates are available for most patchwork designs, but it's far more satisfying and of course cheaper to make your own. Also, if you know the principles of making templates, you will be able to copy designs that you see, such as those in antique quilts.

If you only intend to use a particular template a few times, thin card is adequate. After about 20 tracings, card templates start to

Making templates

become worn and are therefore inaccurate. The most durable materials are metal and plastic. For home use, plastic is better as it can be cut much more easily. Special template plastic, which is transparent and easy to cut and mark, is readily available from art, craft and quilting suppliers.

If you are making templates for hand-pieced work (see page 46, Piecing), you should make them the exact size of the finished piece – i.e., without seam allowances. However, if you are making templates for machine piecing, you should include the seam allowances on your final template.

▲ *It is useful to know how to make your own templates and some quilters enjoy the challenge. Nowadays, however, ready-made templates are available in a wide range of shapes and sizes.*

Making a square template from cardboard

1 *Draw a square of the required size on graph paper. Use a very sharp pencil so that the shape isn't distorted.*

2 *If you are sewing by hand, cut along the marked lines. If you are sewing by machine, add 5 mm ($^1/_4$ in) all around and cut along the outer line.*

3 *Glue the paper square face up on a piece of card, then cut the card around the edges of the paper, using a steel rule and scalpel for accuracy.*

Making a triangular template using template plastic

1 *Draw a triangle of the required size on graph paper. Add seam allowances if necessary.*

2 *Place the plastic over the graph paper and trace the shape. If you have a specialized ruler for cutting triangles (see page 26, Equipment), you can draw onto the plastic.*

3 *Using a scalpel and a steel rule, cut out the template. Keep your fingers away from the cutting edge.*

Making appliqué templates

1 *Draw or trace the shape onto paper, card or template plastic. If you are using a shape that isn't the right size, follow the instructions on page 40 for enlarging or reducing.*

2 *Add 5 mm (¼ in) seam allowance round all the edges of the shape.*

3 *If you are using paper, glue it on card, then cut around the outside line; if you are using template plastic, simply cut around the outside line.*

Making a Dresden Plate template

1 *Draw two straight lines at an angle to each other. The angle will be 360° divided by the number of petals that you want; a 12-petal design needs an angle of 30° (360 ÷ 12).*

2 *From the point, measure out the same distance along both lines. The distance will be half the diameter of the design, so for a 20 cm (8 in) plate, measure 10 cm (4 in) from the corner.*

3 *Join the two marks with a faint line, then draw in a point or a curve depending on the shape you want. Draw an inner curve a short way in from the angle. Add 5 mm (¼ in) seam allowance and cut the shape out.*

The most important thing to remember when you are cutting your fabric into pieces for patchwork is *accuracy*. If your patches aren't cut accurately, they won't fit together properly. The finished piecing may be too large or too small if you have cut the pieces with too much or too little seam allowance.

Make sure that your templates are very precise, checking them against your full-size

Cutting fabrics

pattern. Always use a very sharp pencil for marking your fabric, pressing it tightly against the template so that your line is accurate. A small piece of sandpaper glued to the back of your template will stop it from moving out of position while you are marking – this is also a useful trick if you are using a rotary cutter. Cut exactly on the line you have drawn, not either outside it or inside it.

Before you do any cutting, make sure that you have prepared your fabric by washing, pressing, straightening any raw edges and cutting off the selvedges (this is because the selvedge is more tightly woven than other areas and therefore pulls the fabric slightly). If you are a beginner, you may prefer to mark and cut one piece of fabric at a time, but experienced quilters cut several layers at once if they are using scissors, and up to eight thicknesses of fabric using a rotary cutter.

If you prefer to use scissors, choose a very sharp pair of dressmaking scissors and keep them only for cutting fabric. Never cut paper or card with them; the fibres lie in numerous different directions and blunt the blades very quickly. If you are using a rotary cutter, you will also need a cutting mat and a quilter's transparent ruler (see page 26). Always sheathe the blade of a rotary cutter after use; the blade is very sharp.

ESTIMATING MATERIAL REQUIRED

For an accurate estimate, make a chart with a column for each of your chosen fabrics. Down the left-hand side, list each piece needed for the patchwork, sashing, borders and backing. Now draw each of these requirements on graph paper (you don't need to draw all 96, of course; just draw 2 or 4 and then multiply). Add up all your requirements for each fabric, and you will have exact amounts. It is, however, worth adding a little extra as a safety margin in case you make mistakes.

Pieces Required	Fabric 1	Fabric 2	Fabric 3	Fabric 4	Fabric 5	Fabric 6
Border 82" × 4" 180 × 10cm		2				
Border 62" × 4" 150 × 10 cm		2				
Sashing 82" × 2" 180 × 5cm			3			
Sashing 2" × 12" 5 × 30cm				20		
Square 4" 10cm	24					
Rectangle 2" × 4" 5 × 10cm	96				96	
Triangle 4" 10cm	96					96
Backing 62" × 90" 150 × 228cm						1

Cutting with scissors

1 *For hand piecing, position your template on the fabric and draw around it. Mark a 5 mm (¼ in) seam allowance for each piece and re-position the template.*

2 *For machine piecing, butt the edges of the templates right up to each other and cut along the solid lines, as the seam allowances are included in the templates.*

3 *If you want to cut more than one layer at a time, mark one layer and stack it on top of two or three other pieces. Pin, then cut through all the layers together.*

Cutting with a rotary cutter

1 *To minimize the number of cuts needed, the fabric is first cut into strips. Fold in half lengthwise twice. With a transparent ruler held at right angles to the fold, trim the raw edges.*

2 *Turn the fabric around so that the layers are to the right of the ruler (reverse if you are left-handed). Line up the ruler along the width needed for your strips and cut along the edge.*

3 *Now use your templates or special cutting rulers to cut the strips into squares, rectangles, triangles or parallelograms, as needed.*

GENERAL CUTTING PRINCIPLES

Always mark, or allow for, the largest pieces on your fabric first. So, for instance, mark borders, sashing and large pattern pieces on your fabric before cutting lots of small elements – otherwise you may find that the areas you have left are not the right shape for your larger pieces. Make sure that the grain lines of your fabric are square and position your templates so that the grain line arrow is straight along the grain.
Always mark on the back of your fabrics.

Once you have chosen the fabrics for each part of your patchwork, you need to decide how you are going to join the patches. Piecing may be done by hand or machine and there are advantages to both methods.

If you decide to stitch by hand, you will be able to carry your work with you wherever you go. It will be slower, but you will often find a few moments when you can sew a few patches

Piecing

Pieced quilt with Flying Geese borders

together. It is also easier to 'fudge' a slightly inaccurate seam by hand and make seams meet where they should.

Much more accuracy is needed when you are stitching by machine, but of course it is much faster. More and more quilters are using their machines for piecing – not to mention quilting (see page 56) and embroidery embellishment. In fact, machine piecing has been used for quilts for about 100 years. A design with lots of small pieces is sometimes easier to piece by hand, but the choice is yours entirely.

Before using your machine for piecing, it is a good idea to use a spare piece of fabric to practise stitching an accurate 5 mm ($\frac{1}{4}$ in) seam. Make several parallel rows, using the pressure foot as a guide for spacing them. Or, place a length of masking tape on the throat plate of your machine exactly 5 mm ($\frac{1}{4}$ in) from the needle and use this as your guide.

Each seam should be pressed after it is stitched. The general rule is to press the seam allowance towards the darker fabric; this will stop the extra fabric from showing through lighter patches. With complex patterns where several seams join in one place, you may end up with the bulk of several seam allowances all pressed towards the same piece of fabric; if this happens, you can trim away some of the fabric, or press one seam in a different direction.

Piecing by hand
Your pieces will have been cut with the stitching lines marked (see page 42). Pin the two pieces right sides together and sew with small running stitches along the stitching lines, beginning and ending with a few back stitches for extra strength.

Piecing by machine
Your patches will have been cut with the seam allowance added and with no stitching lines marked. Pin the two pieces right sides together and sew exactly 5 mm ($\frac{1}{4}$ in) away from the edge.

Matching seams

When you need to match the seams of two composite patches, put the fabrics together and then pin across the seam allowances. If you're careful, you should be able to sew across the pin while it is still in place.

Assembly-line method

To save time when you are sewing several sets of patches, put them together in pairs, then stitch them on the machine one after another, without breaking the thread between each pair. When all the seams have been stitched, cut between the pairs.

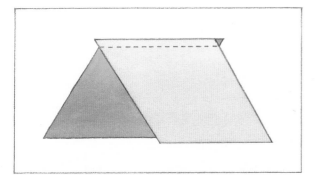

Offset seams

If a seam is between two angled pieces, position them right sides together so that the ends of the seam allowances, rather than the ends of the patches themselves, are aligned.

Joining multiple seams

To get an exact alignment, put a pin through one patch where the seams join, then push it through the seam in the other patch, right sides together. Pin the two patches across the seam allowances, then remove the first pin.

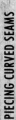

PIECING CURVED SEAMS

Mark the centre of each seam with a pin or a notch. Match the pins or the notches at the centre, right sides together, and pin in position, then pin the ends of the seams. Ease the seam allowances together evenly, pinning at right angles as you go.

Stitch along the seam line by hand or machine, then remove the pins and press the seam allowance towards the darker side. If the seam allowance doesn't lie flat, clip it slightly so that it can be pressed into position.

There are several basic ways of marking quilting patterns. Each method has its pros and cons and some are more suitable for certain fabrics or for certain tasks than others; experiment with the methods shown here and see which ones you find most comfortable.

For making the actual marks on your fabric you can use several different tools. An ordinary medium-hard pencil, sharpened to a

Marking quilting patterns

▼ **A marked quilt pattern**
This is a pattern for a wholecloth cushion cover, marked on the fabric with water-soluble ink to produce a strong line.

good point, will make clear marks, but won't necessarily wash out, so only use this method if you are confident that your stitching will cover all of the pencil marks – for instance, if you are quilting a particular area with chain stitch. Pens with water-soluble ink, which produce strong marks that disappear when moistened, can be extremely useful. Pens with fading ink also produce strong marks which fade sometimes within a few hours, so don't mark a large area at one time! Fading-ink pens are useful if you don't want to have to wet the finished item. Coloured pencils are often ideal for marking plain fabrics; choose a shade just slightly darker than your fabric and sharpen it to a good point. You will find that the marks are unnoticeable when the quilting is complete. Iron-on transfers and transfer pens make a strong mark that doesn't usually wash out, so again make sure that your stitching will cover the line – some quilting patterns use a silver-grey transfer line, which is less noticeable. For marking patterns on stretched plain quilt tops, some people like to use a blunt needle or a silverpoint; these make fine indented lines which, again, are unnoticeable when the quilting is complete.

Tracing around templates
If you are quilting a pattern without any internal lines, or if you have a template with the internal lines cut out, you can simply trace round the shape using pencil or coloured pencil, soluble or fading ink, or a blunt needle or silverpoint.

Tracing through fabric

When your fabric is very pale or very fine, you may be able to trace through it. Lay your pattern face up on a flat surface, place your fabric, right side up, on top and trace the pattern using pencil or coloured pencil, or soluble or fading ink (see page 29).

Light box

If you have access to a designer's light box, it can be used to make a medium-toned fabric more transparent so that you can trace through it. Lay the pattern on the light box with the fabric right side up on top, and trace the pattern.

Prick and pounce

This method is useful for dark fabrics. Perforate your pattern along all the lines with a pin or machine stitching, lay it on top of your fabric and dust chalk or talcum powder through the holes with cotton wool.

Iron-on transfers

Iron-on transfers are available for some patterns and you can also buy transfer pens for drawing your own design on paper. Lay the transfer face down on the right side of the fabric, then press with a warm iron. Remember that the design will be reversed.

Dressmaker's carbon paper

This is available in several different colours, so you can choose a colour that will work well with your fabric. Lay the carbon paper face down on the right side of your fabric and place your pattern on top; run a dressmaker's tracing wheel over all the lines of the pattern.

Blunt needle or silverpoint

This method works best on plain fabrics that have already been stretched taut on a frame. Lay your template down on the right side of your fabric and trace round all the lines with the blunt needle or silverpoint, which will make an indented line on the fabric.

Quilted border designs add interest to a quilt top. They can be added to plain sashings and fabric borders (see page 152) or stitched around the edges of wholecloth projects (see page 100) to provide visual contrast and interest. In many ways working a border design is similar to working with other quilted designs such as individual medallions or background textures; they are marked on to the fabric using

Adding quilted borders

A simple but effective example of a quilted border

the same methods (see page 48) and stitched in the same way by hand or machine (see page 56). However, quilted border designs present some extra challenges to the quilter and you need to plan your border pattern carefully, watching out for some of the common pitfalls.

The first task is to choose your border pattern; you may decide to pick out some elements from your pieced or quilted centre design, such as flower shapes or diamonds, and make a border using those, or you may choose a pattern that contrasts. Most border patterns are made of repeating shapes, and you need to choose a pattern that will fill your border area with whole repeats. If the measurement doesn't quite work out, you may find that you can adjust it by enlarging or reducing the border pattern slightly.

Continuing the border pattern around the corners of the quilt can be a little tricky. Some commercial quilting patterns for borders also include extra templates for corners. If you are making up your own border, you may need to make some sketches first to experiment with different ways of carrying the pattern around the corner. If it proves too difficult, you can finish the edges of the border neatly on each side of the corner and fill the corner itself with a complementary motif or medallion.

The notch method

1 *This method will help you to mark even borders for twisted designs such as cables, using just one small template. Draw your chosen pattern full-size very accurately onto paper; draw several repeats of the basic shape so that you can see exactly where each repeat begins and ends.*

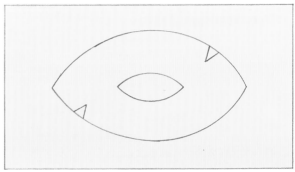

2 *Using either template plastic or sturdy card (see page 42) so that you have a durable surface for marking against, cut the basic template for one repeat of your chosen pattern. Cut or mark a notch on each side of the shape where the next repeat begins.*

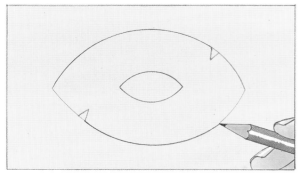

3 Use this template as a guide for marking your fabric. Mark around the long outside edges between the tips of the template and the notches. Mark the inside edge all round.

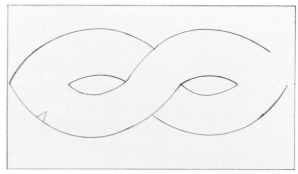

4 Move the template along so that the tips and notches align with the previous marks and mark the next pattern repeat in the same way. Continue this process until the border is as long as you need it.

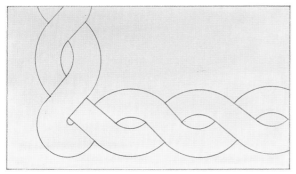

Working with corners

1 If you have a matching corner template, mark it first in one corner and then work outwards along each side to the next corners.

2 If you don't want to take the border around the corner, finish off the border pattern neatly on each side of the corner and fill the space with a complementary motif.

Working with one-way patterns

1 If you are working with a pattern which moves in one direction, for instance a feathered design or a twisted cable, you may want the pattern going in the same direction all the way round the quilt border.

2 If you prefer the quilt design to be symmetrical, work a motif or medallion in the centre of the side of the quilt and mark the border design outwards from this, reversing the template so that each section goes in a different direction. Do the same on the other sides of the quilt.

51

B efore a block, or a whole quilt top, is quilted, a 'sandwich' is made of the top fabric, a padded filling known as wadding, and a backing fabric. Wadding comes in several thicknesses and is made from several different fibres. Polyester is the most popular. It is light, easy to stitch and has the great advantage of being washable. It comes in several different thicknesses, which are usually described by

Wadding and backing

▲ *These examples show the effects of different weights of wadding; the same design has been quilted on the same fabric using 2 oz, 4 oz and 6 oz wadding.*

weight. The most common weights are 2 oz (thin), 4 oz (medium), 6 oz (thick) and 8 oz (extra-thick). If you want something that doesn't quite fall into any of these categories it is possible to combine two weights or to separate the layers of wadding. Dark-coloured polyester wadding can be used behind dark fabrics.

In the past, the type of wadding used generally depended on what material was most readily available in that particular region; so, for example, British quilters tended to use wool whereas North American quilters generally used cotton. In both countries, silk wadding was expensive and kept for very special items. These older types of wadding are becoming popular again for specialized projects; some quilters choose cotton or wool wadding when they want a more compact filling for a quilted item or use a silk wadding to line a silk garment. When you are making a quilted garment, you don't want a lot of bulk, so flatter wadding such as flannelette can be useful. Check the washing instructions on the wadding before you use it, as many silk, cotton and wool waddings can't be machine-washed.

If you don't want your quilting stitches to show on the back of the quilt, use a piece of muslin or a similar fabric as an inner backing while you are quilting, and then attach the final backing fabric.

▲ *This is a wholecloth cushion cover ready for quilting; the fabric has been marked with the quilting pattern and then sandwiched together with wadding and muslin.*

The quilts below show how different backing fabrics work. The one on the left clearly shows the outlines of the *quilting patterns, while the backing fabric on the right almost camouflages the stitches.*

1 To prepare a piece of fabric for quilting, place the ironed backing fabric right side down on a flat surface and smooth it out. If you are quilting a particularly large item, you may need to work on the floor.

2 Place the wadding on top of the backing fabric and smooth out any creases. Place the fabric to be quilted right side up on top of the wadding.

3 Beginning in the centre of the quilt and working out to the edges, pin through all three layers in rows spaced approximately 7.5 cm (3 in) apart.

4 Tack through all three layers in parallel horizontal rows, about 5 cm (2 in) apart. Then tack even rows of stitches vertically, forming a regular grid of tacking across the sandwich of fabrics. This will keep the layers from moving around while you are quilting. Remove the pins.

SAFETY-PIN METHOD

Stitching an even grid of tacking can be time-consuming, and some quilters prefer quicker ways of securing their work. If you are in a hurry, try this method: make the sandwich of backing, wadding and top fabric as above, then secure the three layers together with large safety pins at regular intervals.

When you are quilting by hand or machine, each quilting stitch introduces tension into the work because you are pulling three layers together – the quilt top, the wadding, and the backing. This process produces the slightly gathered effect which gives quilting its attractive texture, but the tension can cause the quilt top to become distorted. To prevent this problem from occurring, handwork is stretched

Quilting frames come in a variety of shapes and sizes

Using a quilting frame

fairly taut while it is being quilted; if your project is small, you may not need to stretch it, but if it is medium-sized or large, you will need some kind of frame.

Hand-held frames don't have any extra means of support and are used for stretching small areas of a quilt at a time. Hand-held frames can be circular or oval; they look like large embroidery frames and are used in the same way, catching the fabric sandwich between an inner and an outer ring.

Floor-standing frames are similar to hand-held frames, but you don't need to support them in your lap or on the edge of a table; they come with their own stands.

Full-size frames are large, free-standing frames which are used for stretching the entire quilt at once. Many quilting groups in the past used flat frames, which made the whole quilt top accessible so that it could be worked on by many quilters simultaneously. These days, few people have sufficient space, so they use a roller frame, an adaptation of the same principle. The quilt top is attached to two rollers and the bulk of the quilt is rolled up onto them, leaving an area exposed for quilting.

When you are quilting by machine, it is difficult to stretch your quilt top in the same way, since few frames will fit under the arm of the machine. If you have an oval frame, it may be useful for stretching machine quilting; if not, use your hands to spread the fabric evenly.

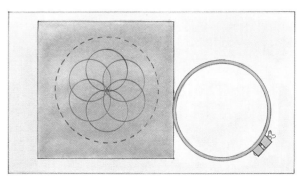

How to use a quilting hoop
1 *Separate the inner and outer hoops of a hand-held or floor-standing frame and lay your tacked quilt sandwich smoothly across the top of the inner hoop.*

2 *Lay the outer hoop over the top layer of fabric so that it catches the quilt top between the two hoops; tighten the tension screw at the side so that the fabric is held firmly between the two rings.*

3 Quilt the area within the hoop, then move the hoop to the adjoining part of the quilt; continue in this way until you have completed the quilting.

4 If you find it difficult to quilt the corner, tack some extra fabric to the edges so that you can stretch it in the frame. When the quilting is complete, remove the extra fabric.

Using a roller frame

1 Lay your quilt sandwich right side up over the frame so that the longer sides are parallel with the flat stretchers at the sides of the frame. Tack the shorter sides of the quilt to the tapes on the rollers.

2 Turn the roller at one end so that it takes up the bulk of the quilt, leaving one end of the quilt top stretched across the frame. Secure the rollers to maintain an even tension.

3 Stretch the sides of the quilt top by winding tape around the stretchers and pinning it in place on the quilt top with large safety pins.

4 Quilt the exposed area of quilt top, then unpin the tape and loosen the rollers. Rewind the rollers until a fresh piece of quilt top appears for stitching, then secure and quilt it in the same way.

Quilting is the stitching you work through the layers of quilt top, wadding and backing fabric. The quilting is functional in that it holds the three layers together, but it is also decorative; as you stitch, you form a textured pattern on the quilt top which enhances your design.

It is possible to work quilting by hand or by machine. Many traditionalists always quilt their quilt tops by hand even if they have pieced

Quilting

them by machine, but there is no reason at all why you shouldn't quilt by machine if you want to. Your stitching will show more, but that isn't necessarily a disadvantage; also, quilting by machine is quicker. Don't worry about how many stitches there are to a couple of centimetres, but practise working stitches of uniform size and tension and you will produce good results. If you are working a long chain or cable design by hand, you may find it useful to work your way along each portion of the pattern using a separate needle and thread for each line, rather than stitching one whole line first and then coming back to do the next one; this helps to keep the tension even.

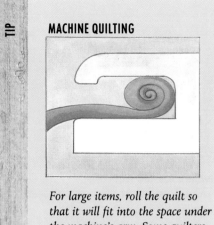

MACHINE QUILTING

For large items, roll the quilt so that it will fit into the space under the machine's arm. Some quilters use bicycle clips to hold the roll.

HAND QUILTING

Use a thimble or thumble (see page 26) on your stitching hand and wind a piece of masking tape around whichever finger you use under the quilt; this will help you to guide the needle tip back up without pricking your finger.

Quilting by machine

1 *Set your machine for a fairly long straight stitch and stitch along the stitching line. To change direction, stop with the needle down, then lift the foot and pivot the fabric.*

2 *If you are quilting long parallel lines, stitch each row in the same direction; otherwise the fabric may show slight puckering marks.*

3 *For quilting intricate designs, attach a darning or embroidery foot and lower the feed dog. Use either an embroidery frame or your hands to keep the fabric stretched and move it freely around.*

top of
the quilt

backing

Quilting by hand

1 Cut a length of thread about 45 cm (18 in) long and thread one end through the eye of your quilting needle. Tie a small knot at the longer end of your thread.

2 Put the needle into the fabric, on the right side, about 2.5 cm (1 in) away from the beginning of your quilting line.

3 Bring your needle up at the beginning of the stitching line and pull gently. The knot will pop down under the surface fabric and stay in the wadding.

4 Sew with small, even running stitches, making sure that you go through all the layers of the quilt. Take several stitches at a time on your needle before you pull it through.

5 When you are near the end of your thread, wind it round the needle twice and draw the knot close to the fabric.

6 Insert the needle into the stitching line, making sure that you draw the knot down into the wadding. Then pull the needle back through the fabric about 2.5 cm (1 in) from the end of the stitching and cut the thread.

PROS AND CONS

Machine quilting

Hand quilting

Machine quilting: pros
It is very quick, so your project takes shape rapidly. It is useful for large, regular patterns.

Specialized accessories such as quilting guides make the stitching very accurate and even.

Machine quilting: cons
You can't carry your work with you. It is harder to keep layers wrinkle-free. The stitching shows more on the right side. Large quilts are difficult to manipulate under the arm of the machine.

Hand quilting: pros
It is attractive because the stitching shows less. It is easier to 'fudge' difficult areas of a design. It creates a soothing rhythm. You can carry small pieces with you to stitch.

Hand quilting: cons
It is very time-consuming. It requires short lengths (46 cm/18 in) of thread, so you are constantly rethreading needles. Long sessions lead to sore hands, pricked fingers and tired eyes.

If you are quilting patchwork or appliqué designs, you can often use the patchwork or appliqué patterns themselves as starting points for your quilting design. The seam lines on pieced work and the edges of appliqué pieces can be followed or echoed by your lines of stitching. Or, if you prefer, you can quilt a traditional or modern design over the top of the pieced work, ignoring the lines made by the

Different ways of quilting blocks

fabric patches, or combine the two techniques, perhaps by quilting small motifs inside some of the patches. Here you can see several ways of quilting the same pieced block, the Churn Dash; all of these methods can be done by hand or by machine.

On this quilt, the shapes of the fabric patches have been used to suggest shapes for quilted patterns and spirals. Along the border, triangles and points have been built up with rows of quilting stitches at different angles.

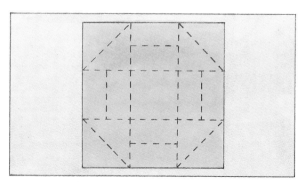

Quilting 'in the ditch' is probably the fastest and the simplest method of quilting patchwork: stitch just next to the seam, on the side away from the seam allowance.

Outline quilting is done on each patch: stitch a row of quilting stitches 5 mm (¼ in) inside each patch, being careful to avoid the seam allowance.

On this block, small individual motifs have been quilted inside some of the patches. This method can be combined very effectively with quilting in the ditch.

Here, the lines of the patchwork design have been ignored completely and the whole block has been quilted over with concentric circles, adding tiny circles in the corners.

Here, the corners of the patchwork pieces have been used as guides for straight lines of quilting intersecting at the centres of the pieces.

This design uses straight lines of quilting stitched diagonally across the outside and central fabric pieces and keeping the same direction each time.

QUILTING APPLIQUE BLOCKS

Hawaiian quilts often use a method known as 'echo quilting', where rows of quilting 5 mm ($\frac{1}{4}$ in) apart follow the outlines of the appliqué design, filling in the spaces with flowing lines.

Background textures are popular for adding visual interest to appliqué blocks and quilt tops. The first line of quilting is worked close to the edge of the appliqué design or 5 mm ($\frac{1}{4}$ in) outside it, then the background fabric is quilted with a geometric or random design to throw the appliqué into relief.

Once your quilt top has been quilted, the edges must be finished and usually some kind of binding is used. For bed quilts, which will be subjected to quite a bit of wear, a good straight binding in a hard-wearing fabric is acceptable, but the ideal edging is bias binding – even better, a double thickness of bias binding. The first part of a quilt to show wear is usually the edge. If a straight binding is used,

Finishing quilts

the single thread at the outside edge can disintegrate, making it necessary to replace the binding. Bias edges are composed of many threads criss-crossing around the whole perimeter of the quilt, so they are far less likely to wear out quickly. A bias binding is also quite elastic and can be coaxed along curves and around corners.

The fabric you choose for your binding should coordinate with the fabrics in the quilt and, although bias binding can be bought in several widths, it is usually better to make your own. Cutting bias strips takes a great deal of fabric and you will need to allow for this when you are buying the fabrics for a quilt. If you are binding a large quilt, sheeting is strong and is very wide, so it is useful for straight and bias bindings. A pieced binding can be made using all the fabrics from the quilt; this is particularly effective if your quilt top has a wide plain border or sashing.

Many quilters bind their quilts by using either the backing or the quilt top to cover the raw edges. If you decide to do this, remember to make the backing or the quilt top about 2.5 cm (1 in) wider all round than the finished size of the quilt. The edges of the quilt are then pressed under, turned to the front or back of the quilt as appropriate, and stitched down. An even simpler way of finishing a quilt top is to trim away about 5 mm ($\frac{1}{4}$ in) of the wadding, turn in the edges of the quilt front and back and stitch them together close to the edge.

A well-made quilt is a work of art to be proud of, so you might think about finishing it off with your name or initials, as artists do. Or, if it's intended as a gift, embroider the name of the recipient. This is a 'friendship quilt', with the names commemorating two women's shared experiences.

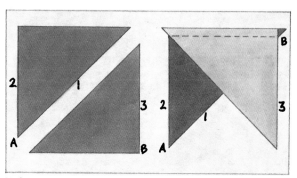

Making a continuous bias strip
1   *Take 1 m (1$\frac{1}{8}$ yd) of 115 cm (45 in) wide fabric. Remove the selvedges and press the fabric. Fold the square across the diagonal and cut; you now have two large triangles. With the right sides together, place two of the short edges together as shown and machine a 5 mm ($\frac{1}{4}$ in) seam.*

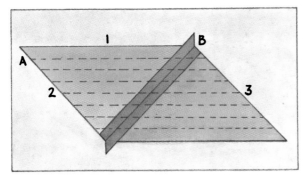

2 Open out the piece and press the seam open; you now have a parallelogram. Mark the desired width of your strip along edge 1, allowing for turning under the edges.

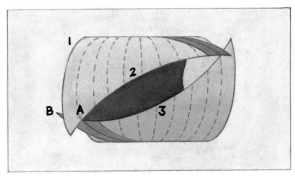

3 Cut a few centimetres along this line; then, with the right sides together, join side 2 to side 3, matching points A and B. Stitch a 5 mm (¼ in) seam to form a tube; the end of side 3 will extend slightly at the end of the tube.

4 Using the cut piece as a width guide, continue cutting around the tube until you reach the end. You will now have a long length of bias binding which can be used to edge your quilt.

5 If you have to join a bias strip, put the right sides together as shown and stitch a narrow seam either by hand or by machine.

Making a straight binding

1 Cut two strips 6 cm (2½ in) wide by the length of the quilt and two strips 6 cm (2½ in) wide by the width of the quilt plus 2.5 cm (1 in). Fold the strips in half lengthwise and press the fold.

2 Lay the longer strips face down along the longer edges of the quilt top; pin and sew them in position about 5 mm (¼ in) from the edges.

3 Turn the strips over to the back of the quilt and turn under the raw edges; stitch into position by hand. Finish the other edges of the quilt the same way.

3

The sampler quilt

Now that you are familiar with the basic principles of making a quilt, it's time to put your knowledge into practice. This section will take you through all the steps necessary for making a sampler quilt, from cutting and piecing to binding the edges of your finished quilt. As you work your way through each lesson, you will be increasing your practical understanding of the piecing, quilting and

Introduction to the sampler quilt

▼ *These are swatches of the fabrics used in the sampler quilt. To make it easier to identify which fabric is being used in each part, each one has been given a letter. We have also given a brief description of the fabrics, all of which are medium-weight 100% cotton.*

finishing techniques. We have chosen traditional blocks and quilting designs so that once you have finished the sampler quilt, you will have mastered most of the basic techniques needed for producing a wide variety of other traditional quilt designs.

In each lesson, you will find cross-references to the relevant pages in the Pattern Library in case you want to substitute one design for another. Remember that amounts of the different fabrics may need to be adjusted if you decide to alter the blocks or borders significantly.

All of the quilting on the sampler quilt can be done by hand or by machine, so you can choose the method which suits you best – or use a mixture of the two methods.

To complement the traditional design of the sampler quilt, we have chosen a traditional colour scheme of pinky reds, grey-greens and creams. You may decide to choose a totally different colour scheme. If so, choose fabrics that have similar values (see page 32) to the ones shown here (so, for instance, your new fabric A would be dark, while your new fabric B would be a lighter version of the same colour). Simply substitute the appropriate fabric each time the relevant letter is mentioned.

Before you start the quilt, wash your fabrics (see page 30) to check that they are colourfast and to pre-shrink them. If necessary, pull the fabrics to straighten the grain; then press them so that they are ready to be cut.

Fabric A
Dark pink background with a small, light green flower-sprig pattern.

Fabric B
Light pink background with a small all-over pattern in white.

Fabric C
Plain dark green.

Fabric D
Light green background with small flower-sprig design in pink.

Fabric E
Plain medium green.

Fabric F
Plain light-to-medium pink.

Fabric G
Unbleached calico.

The nine blocks of the sampler quilt have been numbered for ease of reference and to correspond with the templates on pages 66-71.

1 *The Four-patch block (see page 72)*

9 *The Reverse Appliqué block (see page 88)*

3 *The Sugar Bowl block (see page 76)*

Sashing (see page 90)

Pieced border (see 11; page 92)

Binding (see 14; page 98)

7 *The Star block (see page 84)*

8 *The Flying Geese block (see page 86)*

4 *The Appliqué block (see page 78)*

6 *The Strip-pieced block (see page 82)*

5 *The Log Cabin block (see page 80)*

◄ *Backing*

Quilted repeat pattern

2 *The Nine-patch block (see page 74)*

Quilted corner motif

MATERIALS REQUIRED

To make the sampler quilt, you will need the following amounts; all of the fabrics are 150 cm (60 in) wide. The measurements given here should give you slightly more than you need, to allow for occasional mistakes while marking or cutting; if you have large pieces left over, you could always make a cushion cover to go with the quilt.

Fabric A: 0.7 m (¾ yd)
Fabric B: 0.7 m (¾ yd)
Fabric C: 0.7 m (¾ yd)
Fabric D: 0.7 m (¾ yd)
Fabric E: 0.7 m (¾ yd)
Fabric F: 0.7 m (¾ yd)
Fabric G: 7.3 m (8 yds)

You will also need:

2 reels of ordinary sewing thread in ecru.
1 piece of medium-weight wadding 200×200 cm (78×78 in).
Quilting thread in green, pink and ecru if you are quilting by hand, or sewing thread in your chosen colours if you are quilting by machine.
1 water-soluble marking pen.
Quilting needle if you are quilting by hand.
A rotary cutter and cutting board.
See pages 26-29 for general equipment for making templates, cutting and sewing.

On these and the following pages you will find all the templates that you will need for the pieced blocks and the quilting patterns that make up the sampler quilt. All of the templates are full-size, so copy each of them carefully onto paper, cardboard, or template plastic (see page 42) and use them as cutting guides. All the seam allowances are included and are $\frac{1}{4}$ in. unless indicated otherwise. The arrows on

Sampler quilt templates

some templates mark the straight grain of the fabric; the arrows should be lined up with either the warp or the weft threads on your fabrics. The blocks which don't require templates have full instructions in the appropriate lesson.

The Four-patch block
Template 1

Grain line

The Nine-patch block
Template 2:2

Grain line

The Nine-patch block
Template 2:1

Each template is identified by the name of the block followed by the number of the block. For blocks that have more than one template, the block number is followed by the appropriate template number.

Grain line

The Nine-patch block
Template 2:3

Grain line

The Sugar Bowl block
Template 3:1

Grain line

The Sugar Bowl block
Template 3:2

Grain line

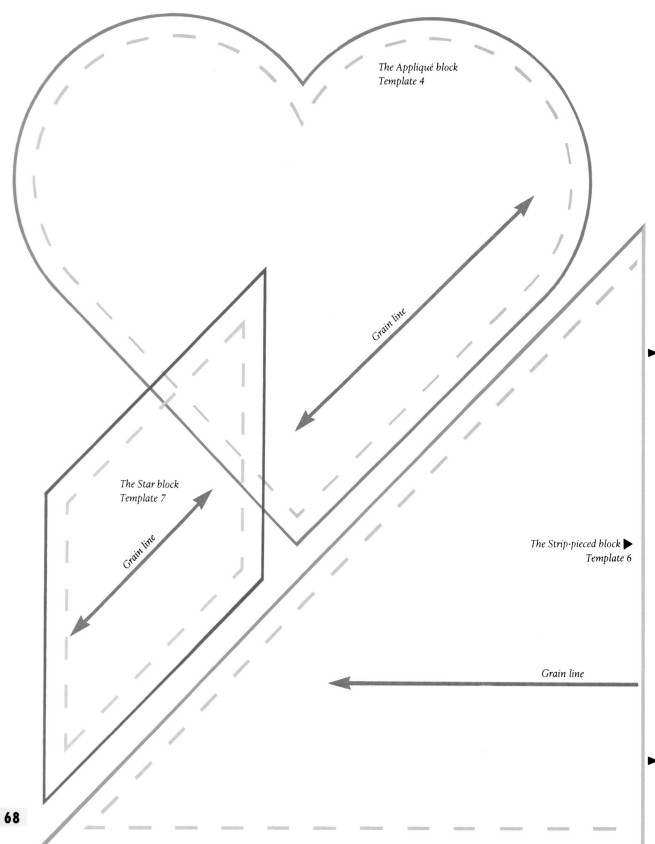

The Appliqué block
Template 4

Grain line

The Star block
Template 7

Grain line

The Strip-pieced block ▶
Template 6

Grain line

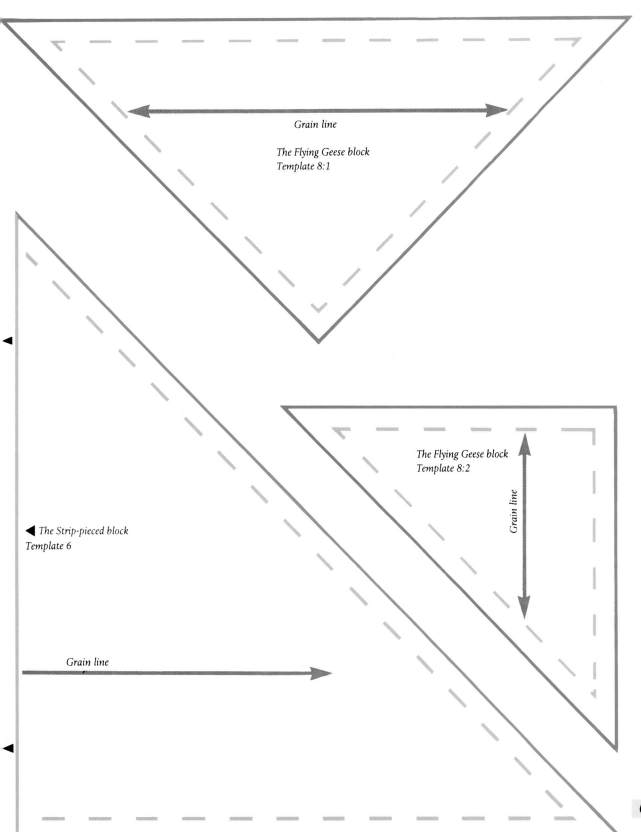

Grain line

The Flying Geese block
Template 8:1

The Flying Geese block
Template 8:2

Grain line

◀ The Strip-pieced block
Template 6

Grain line

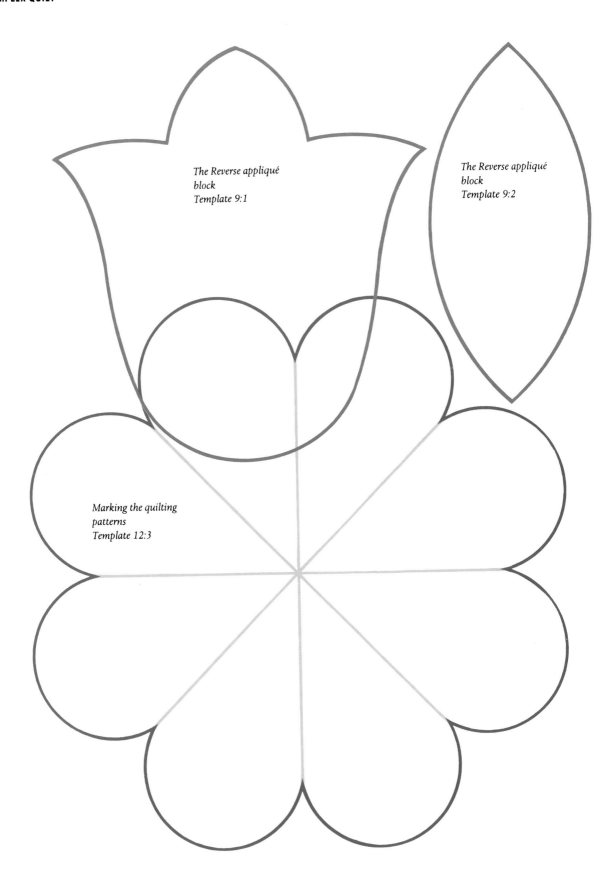

*The Reverse appliqué
block
Template 9:1*

*The Reverse appliqué
block
Template 9:2*

*Marking the quilting
patterns
Template 12:3*

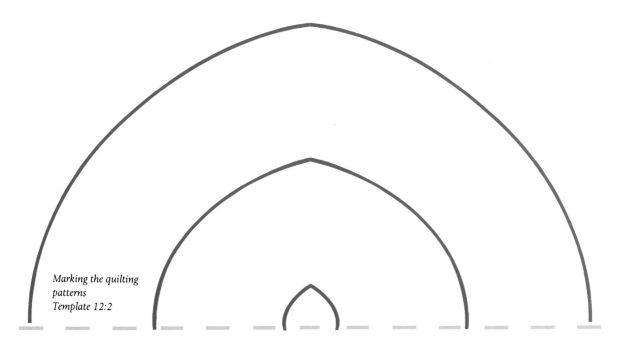

*Marking the quilting
patterns
Template 12:2*

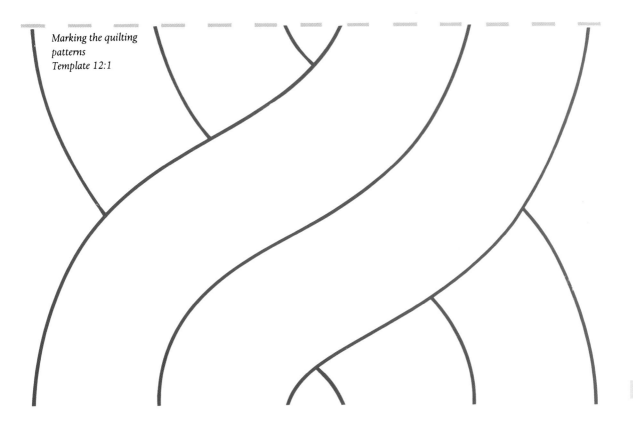

*Marking the quilting
patterns
Template 12:1*

What exactly is a four-patch block? As its name suggests, it is a square design that is divisible into four separate basic patches, or units, which are constructed one at a time before being stitched together to form the complete block. There are many variations of four-patch blocks and a selection is shown in the Pattern Library (page 122). In this lesson you'll learn how to construct the block called Rail

1

1 The Four-patch block

Fence, which is a simple four-patch design. Only two fabrics are used in this and only one template, but the way that the fabrics are alternated, with two of the patches turned on their sides, makes an attractive block design.

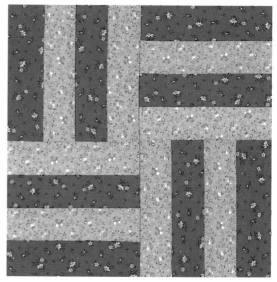

▲ The alternating colours produce a dramatic effect from a very simple pattern.

IDENTIFYING A FOUR-PATCH BLOCK

This might seem self-evident, but some designs which seem to divide neatly into quarters are actually more complex. A design is a standard four-patch block if you can divide it into four quarters without cutting into any of the shaped pieces.

This is a four-patch design.

This is a four-patch design.

This is not a four-patch design.

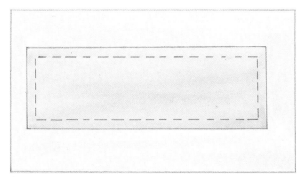

1 Trace template 1 on page 66 full-size onto a piece of thin card and cut it out very accurately (see page 40, Making templates). Also mark the seam allowance lines and the grain line.

2 Using the template as a guide, cut eight pieces from fabric A and eight pieces from fabric D. Make sure that you position the template each time so that the marked grain line lies either horizontally or vertically along the straight grain of the fabric.

3 Take one piece of fabric A and one piece of fabric D and place them right sides together. Stitch a 5 mm (¼ in) seam along one of the long edges by hand or machine (see page 46, Piecing) and press the seam towards the darker fabric. Repeat with the seven remaining pairs of pieces.

4 Take two pairs of patches and place them right sides together so that the edge of fabric A on one piece is against the edge of fabric D on the other. Join this seam and press it to the darker side to form one of the four basic patches for the block. Repeat three times to make the other three patches.

5 Take one patch and turn it 90° so that the strips are horizontal. Right sides together, join it in the same way to the side of another patch turned so the strips are vertical. Press the seam open. Repeat for the other patches.

6 Join the two halves together as shown to complete the blocks and press the seam open. You now have a complete Rail Fence block.

As the name implies, nine-patch blocks are divided into nine sections, which are joined first in rows of three; then three rows are joined to form the whole block. Nine-patch blocks are exciting to work with because the larger number of patches offers more variety in the designs. Nine-patch block designs often have a blank square in the centre, which can be a focal point for a splash of colour or some form

2 _____

2 The Nine-patch block

of fancy quilted embellishment. We have chosen the Churn Dash block for the second block of our sampler quilt. It is based on an even grid of nine squares, it needs only three templates and it will give you practice in stitching diagonal seams.

As with many other blocks, a nine-patch often has several names. Churn Dash and Hole in the Barn Door are sometimes called Wrench, and Jack in the Box is also known as Double Z. Some nine-patch designs, such as Bear's Paw and Hole in the Barn Door, have the block divided slightly differently from the basic nine-patch, in that the central section of the grid is narrower than the outer sections, but many nine-patch designs are based on a grid of nine equal squares.

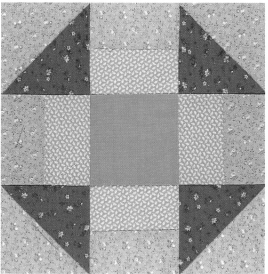

▲ The finished block, showing an interesting interplay among the different fabrics.

The most regular nine-patch blocks are made up of nine equal squares (a), so they are easy to recognize. However, more complex blocks may also be nine-patch designs. The test is whether you can construct them into three straight rows of three blocks, regardless of the widths of the blocks; designs b and c are both still nine-patch blocks, even though they look very different to traditional ones.

a

Basic nine-patch.

b

Bear's Paw variation.

c

Card Trick design.

74

1 Make templates 2:1, 2:2 and 2:3 on page 66. Using template 2:1 cut one piece from fabric C (see page 44, Cutting fabrics). Using template 2:2, cut four pieces from fabric B and four from fabric D. Using template 2:3, cut four pieces from fabric A and four from fabric D.

2 Following the instructions on page 46 (Piecing), join the light green (fabric D) triangles to the dark pink (fabric A) triangles along the long edge, right sides together, taking care not to stretch the fabric as you stitch. This gives you four identical square patches, called unit **a**.

3 Right sides together join the light green (fabric D) rectangles to the light pink (fabric B) rectangles along one long edge. This will give you four more identical square patches, called unit **b**.

4 Join two unit **a** patches to the edges of one unit **b** patch. Position the patches so that the light green triangles and the light green rectangle are all at the top of the new design. Repeat to make two identical strips.

5 Join the two remaining unit **b** patches to the edges of the dark green (fabric C) square, making sure that the light pink rectangles are next to the square on both sides. This makes the central row of the block.

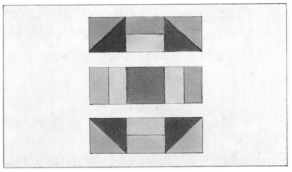

6 Join the three rows, making sure that the light pink rectangles of the top and bottom strips are next to the green central square. You now have a Churn Dash block.

Like the Rail Fence block (see page 72), this block is a four-patch design made in four even, square patches. This one, however, uses two templates and also introduces curved seams. Curved seams introduce exciting new dimensions into quilt patterns, because they take the eye away from the grid structure of the block and allow it to be drawn across the work to follow the curved lines. On page 130 you will

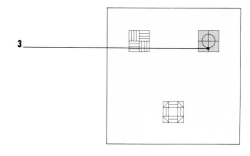

3 _____

3 The Sugar Bowl block

SAMPLER QUILT

find ways in which you can combine Sugar Bowl blocks to make more complex patterns such as Drunkard's Path where, as the name suggests, the curves weave to and fro across the quilt top. Here, though, we are making only one block; the light/dark contrast between the green and pink produces a strong design using just two different fabrics.

▼ *The finished block, showing a strong contrast between the two fabrics.*

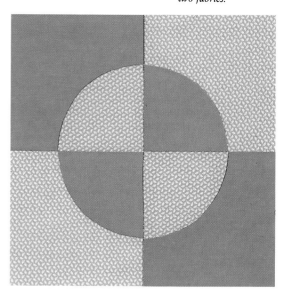

CUTTING CURVED SEAMS

When you are cutting out your fabric it is very important to make sure that any curved edges are smooth. Cut them carefully with scissors or use a rotary cutter against a strong template. It is important to have a strong template so that you don't cut into the template itself.

1 *Make templates 3:1 and 3:2 on page 67. Using template 3:1, cut two pieces from fabric B and two from fabric C. Using template 3:2, cut two pieces from fabric B and two from fabric C.*

76

2 Following the instructions on page 47 for curved seams, stitch the curved edges of the pink (fabric B) quarter-circles inside the edges of the large green (fabric C) pieces.

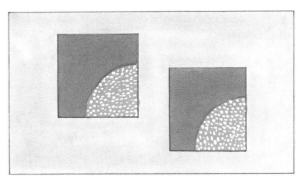

3 Open out the pieces to the right side. You now have two identical patches, unit **a**.

4 Using the same method, stitch the green (fabric C) quarter-circles to the curved edges of the large pink (fabric B) pieces. You now have two more patches, unit **b**.

5 Stitch one unit **a** to one unit **b**, matching the seams carefully so that you get a smooth half-circle.

6 Stitch the other two units **a** and **b** together to form an identical half-block.

7 Matching the seams carefully at the edges and in the centre, stitch the two half-blocks together so that you have a complete circle in the centre of the block.

Appliqué can be worked by hand or machine. When you appliqué by machine, it is impossible to hide the stitching completely. You can achieve a low-key effect by turning under the edges of the shapes and applying them with a single line of machine straight stitch or you can capitalize on the machine stitching and cover the raw edges by stitching around the edges of the shapes with satin stitch or a close

4

4 The Appliqué block

zigzag. When you stitch by hand, you can choose whether to make the stitching nearly invisible or part of the decorative effect by using blanket, feather or a variety of other embroidery stitches.

On this block we show you how to turn the edges under and tack them before you position the motifs. When you get more proficient, you may prefer to use the quicker turn-as-you-go method – the shapes are simply pinned in place and you turn under the seam allowance as you stitch around the edges of the shape. Another method involves cutting the required shapes from freezer paper and sticking the edges under by pressing them to the tacky wax layer; the appliqué is stitched to the background fabric, then a slit is cut behind the appliqué to remove the paper.

▲ *The completed block, a simple design of hearts in green fabrics set off by the pink background.*

 TIP

When you are sewing by hand, your thread can easily become tangled and form small knots. There is nothing more irritating than this, but you can prevent it by running the thread across a lump of beeswax. The coating of wax must be quite light, however, or it may discolour the fabric.

1 *Trace template 4 on page 68 and cut a heart template for the appliqué pieces (see page 42, Making templates).*

2 *Using the template, cut two hearts from fabric C and two from fabric D (see page 44, Cutting fabrics).*

3 *Fold and tack under 5 mm (¹/₄ in) all round the edges of the heart shapes. Clip to the seam allowance at the top of each heart so that the fabric folds under smoothly. Keep the curves smooth round the edges of each shape.*

4 *Cut a 31.75 cm (12¹/₂ in) square from fabric F and fold it lightly across the diagonals, so that you have some guidelines for positioning your appliqué shapes.*

5 *Pin or tack the heart shapes in position on the background fabric so that there are even borders of the pink (fabric F) square round the edges of the hearts.*

6 *Using green sewing thread, blind-stitch the hearts to the background fabric by taking tiny hemming stitches around the edges of the shapes. Remove the pins or tacking thread. To reduce bulk you can cut away some of the background fabric behind the heart shapes.*

og Cabin is one of the most exciting and versatile of all patchwork designs. It can be made in two colours or fifty colours; any fabric can be used; the strips may be any width you choose; and once several blocks are completed, they can be arranged in many different ways to make an endless variety of designs. Even the ways in which the strips are attached can be varied. The Log Cabin designs in the Pattern

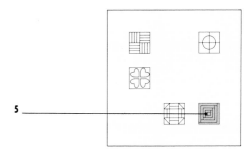

5 —————

5 The Log Cabin block

▼ *The finished Log Cabin block, half dark and half light to represent night and day.*

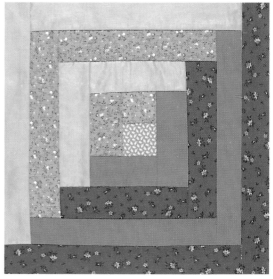

Library (pages 136-139) show just a few of the myriad possibilities open to you.

To introduce you to the basic principle of Log Cabin, which is different from other methods of patchwork, we are using a standard block which makes use of five different fabrics.

To make the block, you will need strips of each fabric 4.75 cm ($1\frac{5}{16}$ in) wide; if you find this measurement difficult to achieve accurately, cut your strips 5 cm (2 in) wide and then take 5 mm ($\frac{1}{4}$ in) for your seam allowance as you stitch each seam. The strips are best cut using a rotary cutter and board (see page 44, Cutting fabrics).

1 *From fabrics A and F, cut strips measuring 4.75 cm ($1\frac{5}{16}$ in) across; you will need a length of about 36 cm (14 in) of each fabric, but this doesn't all need to be in one piece. From fabrics C and D, cut strips the same width and a total of 90 cm (36 in) in length for each. Cut along the grain.*

2 *From fabric G, cut a 31.75 cm ($12\frac{1}{2}$ in) square. Fold the square in half diagonally and then in half again and press lightly; unfold it and you will have your diagonals marked, which will help you to keep the strips straight.*

3 From fabric B cut a 4.75 cm (1⅞ in) square and pin it in the exact centre of the large fabric square, using the pressed lines as a guide for positioning it.

4 Cut a strip from fabric D the same width as the small square and lay it face down over the square so that the two raw edges align. Stitch a 5 mm (¼ in) seam by hand or machine.

5 Fold the fabric strip open so that the right side is uppermost and press the seam.

6 Cut another strip of fabric D, this time long enough to go across the square and the edge of the first strip, and attach to the next edge around in the same way.

7 Attach strips of fabric C to the remaining two sides in the same way. Continuing to work around the square in the same direction, add two strips of fabric F and then two strips of fabric A in the same way to make the next round. As you work your way outwards on the block, you need longer and longer strips.

8 Finish off the block with another round of strips D and C and a final round of strips F and A. Make sure that you stitch around the block in the same order for every round.

S trip piecing is a marvellous time-saver that enables you to produce very sophisticated results quickly.

In strip piecing, strips are cut from different fabrics, sometimes in varying widths, and joined together along their lengths before being cut into the required patches. If you don't have a sewing machine it is perfectly possible to do strip piecing by hand, but it is much

6 ——

6 The Strip-pieced block

faster to do the stitching by machine. Cutting the fabrics with a rotary cutter (see page 44, Cutting fabrics) is very quick and accurate, but if you prefer, the fabrics can be cut in the conventional way with scissors. This block uses even strips of six different fabrics.

If you cut your fabric strips to different widths before they are pieced and reassembled, the finished block has a more random effect.

▲ *The finished block. Piecing the strips in this way gives the effect of several squares of fabric inside one another.*

String piecing

String piecing evolved as a way of using up long narrow pieces of fabric left over after cutting out garments. These 'strings' are often irregularly shaped, but by trimming them into long triangles and sewing them together you can make a new fabric which can then be cut up and used for quilt patches or for garments. Stitch the strings onto a backing of thin fabric using the 'face-down, fold-back' method shown on page 80 (the Log Cabin block.)

1 *Cut two strips of fabric, each 71 cm (28 in) long and 3.8 cm (1½ in) wide, from each of fabrics A, B, C, D, E and F.*

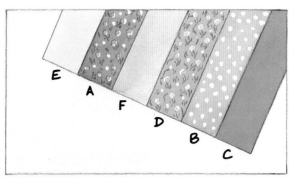

2 *Following the method for piecing (see page 46), join one set of fabric strips along their long edges in the order E, A, F, D, B, C. Do the same with the other set of strips; you now have two identical lengths of strip-pieced fabric.*

3 *Make a template using template 6 on page 68 (see also page 42, Making templates).*

4 *Use the template to cut two triangles from each length of strip-pieced fabric, laying the long edge of the triangle 5 mm (¼ in) in from the raw edge of fabric E each time.*

5 *Stitch two of the triangles together along one short seam, matching the fabrics and making sure that the seam lines match exactly. Stitch the other two triangles together in the same way to form two identical half-blocks.*

6 *Stitch the two half-blocks together along their long edges, matching the fabrics and the seam lines exactly, to complete the block.*

Diamonds can be used to produce wonderful star shapes simply by stitching them around in a circle. As you can see from the examples on page 132 (Non-block patterns), the stars can become quite spectacular; the Star of Bethlehem pattern is very dramatic and can be made large enough to cover a whole double quilt top. This star is a little more modest, to get you used to using diamonds in a star

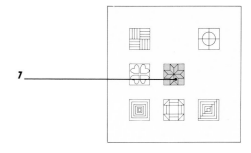

SAMPLER QUILT

7 The Star block

arrangement. When the basic star has been pieced, it is appliquéd by hand to the background fabric to make a block.

The number of points your star has is determined by the acute angle at the tip of the diamond; this star uses 45° diamonds, so the star has eight points (360° divided by 45°). The use of the two pink fabrics, one light and one dark, arranged in pairs, gives a three-dimensional look to the finished star. If you want to make stars with six points, then you need to use 60° diamonds (360° ÷ 6). It is possible to create stars with even more points, but if the angle becomes too fine it is difficult to piece the diamonds accurately, so six-point and eight-point designs tend to be the most popular.

> **TIP**
> For the star to look effective, each point must be really sharp and crisp. It is easier to tack sharp points if you trim away some of the excess fabric. Cut across the top of the point and turn it down. Then turn down one side followed by the other.

▼ *The finished block shows a good contrast between dark, light and middle tones.*

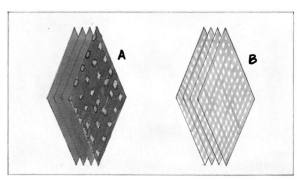

1 *Make template 7 on page 68 (see page 42, Making templates) and use it to cut four pieces from fabric A and four pieces from fabric B.*

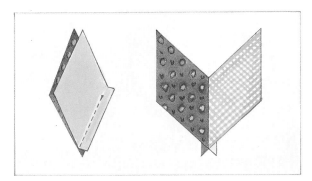

2 *Take one diamond in fabric A and one in fabric B and put them right sides together. Following the instructions on page 46 (Piecing), stitch down one edge so that side **a** of the fabric A diamond is joined to side **b** of the fabric B diamond.*

3 *Do the same with the remaining pairs of diamonds so that you have four identical V-shaped patches. On all the seams, leave the top open for the first 5 mm (¼ in); this will make it easier to turn under the seam allowances later.*

4 *Place two of the patches right sides together and stitch down the right-hand lower edge to form a half-star. Once again, leave the top 5 mm (¼ in) of the seam open.*

5 *Do the same with the remaining two patches; you now have two identical half-stars.*

6 *Place the two half-stars right sides together and stitch a straight seam across them. Leave this seam open for 5 mm (¼ in) at each end.*

7 *Tack under the 5 mm (¼ in) seam allowances on the edges of the star. Following the instructions on page 78 (Appliqué block), stitch the star by hand on to the centre of a 31.75 cm (12½ in) square of fabric E. You now have an eight-point star block for your quilt top.*

This delicate block, made in two basic pieces, is a variation on the traditional pattern known as Flying Geese, which always features a pattern of right-angled triangles arranged in the same direction. The 'geese' can be made to fly all around the block or entirely in one direction across it or around a border (see page 150, Pieced border patterns). Here, one gaggle flies south and the other gaggle north!

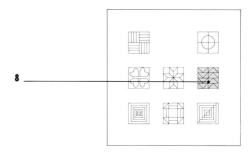

8

8 The Flying Geese block

SAMPLER QUILT

This is the most complex block for your sampler quilt and you need to be very accurate when you are making the templates (see page 42) and cutting out the fabric (see page 44). A quilter's ruler for right-angled triangles will come in handy for cutting your shapes.

▼ *The finished block, showing foursomes of 'geese' flying in different directions.*

USING A QUILTER'S MAT

Cutting a strip of fabric will be much more accurate if you cut it with a rotary cutter and a quilter's ruler or a rotary cutter and a mat used for cutting triangles. Cut a strip of fabric the width of one of the perpendicular edges of the small triangles, then use the 45° angle guide to cut the triangles across it. Repeat for the larger triangles, using the larger template and a wider strip of fabric.

1 *Make triangular templates 8:1 and 8:2 on page 69. Using template 8:1, cut eight shapes from fabric D. Using template 8:2, cut 16 shapes from fabric F.*

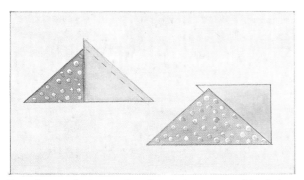

2 *Following the instructions for piecing on page 46, stitch the long side of one pink (fabric F) triangle to the right-hand diagonal of one green (fabric D) triangle. Repeat the procedure for the other green (fabric D) triangles and press all the seams.*

3 *Stitch the long side of one pink (fabric F) triangle to the other diagonal of each green (fabric D) triangle. You now have eight identical rectangles.*

4 *Stitch the rectangles together in two groups of four, making sure that the green triangles point in the same direction in each group. Stitch the seams so that the point of one triangle just touches the base of the next.*

5 *From fabric A, cut three strips 2 cm ($^3/_4$ in) wide and 30 cm (12 in) long, and two strips 2 cm ($^3/_4$ in) wide and 31.75 cm ($12^1/_2$ in) long.*

6 *Stitch one of the shorter strips between the half-blocks, taking a 5 mm ($^1/_4$ in) seam on each side and making sure that the green triangles point in different directions in each half. Stitch the other two short strips to the outside edges of the rectangles.*

7 *Stitch the longer strips to the top and bottom of the block, again taking 5 mm ($^1/_4$ in) seams. You now have a complete Flying Geese block.*

This block introduces a new technique, reverse appliqué. Instead of stitching fabric shapes on top of a background fabric as you did for the appliqué block earlier, the second fabric is laid underneath the background, which is then cut away in shapes to reveal it.

Just as conventional appliqué gives a slightly puffed or three-dimensional look to the shapes applied onto the flat background fabric,

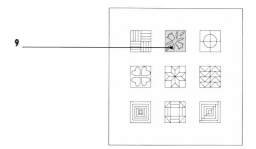

SAMPLER QUILT

9 The Reverse appliqué block

this method gives a slightly puffed look to the top layer of fabric as it is turned and stitched over flat areas of fabric shapes.

There are many methods of reverse appliqué and variations within the methods themselves, but this block uses one of the simplest. Use this method for virtually any conventional appliqué designs (see page 134) to vary the final effect.

A well-known form of reverse appliqué is that produced by the Indian women of Panama's San Blas Islands. Their traditional dress includes a sleeveless blouse called a mola, with reverse appliqué panels on both front and back. These colourful and intricate panels have semi-naturalistic designs based on plants, people and creatures or tales from local folklore. Several layers of different-coloured fabric are used; empty spaces are often filled with lines of plain stitching or embroidery.

► *The finished block: the red tulip shapes and dark green leaves produce a pretty pattern on the light green background.*

1 *Make templates 9:1 and 9:2 on page 70. From fabric D, cut a 31.75 cm (12½ in) square; this will be your background fabric. Make a soft diagonal fold across the square to divide it into two large triangles; this will help you position the templates accurately on both sides.*

2 *Mark the tulip and leaf shapes on the background square by drawing around with a soft pencil, positioning them so that each diagonal half is a mirror image of the other. Make sure that the shapes are at least 1.25 cm (^{1}/$_2$ in) from the edges of the square.*

3 *Using small, sharp scissors, cut 5 mm (^{1}/$_4$ in) inside each of the pencil lines and carefully clip any curves; clip into the corners of the shapes also.*

4 *Using the tulip template as a rough guide, cut two shapes from fabric A that are at least 1.25 cm (^{1}/$_2$ in) larger all around than the template.*

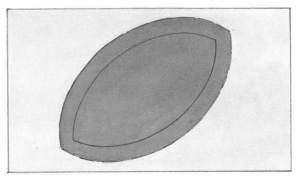

5 *Using the leaf template as a rough guide, cut six shapes from fabric C that are at least 1.25 cm (^{1}/$_2$ in) larger all around than the template.*

6 *Tack the dark pink (fabric A) pieces, face up, underneath the tulip-shaped holes in the background fabric. Tack the dark green (fabric C) pieces behind the leaf-shaped holes in the same way.*

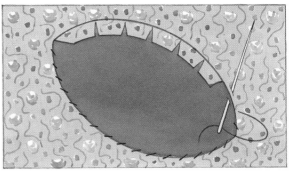

7 *Roll under the raw edges of the background fabric until the pencil line is just hidden, and blind-stitch the background fabric to the coloured shapes underneath. Keep the curves of the rolled fabric smooth so that each piece of reverse appliqué makes a pleasing shape.*

89

You now have nine blocks for your sampler quilt and it is time to put them together. This stage turns your work from a collection of blocks into a real quilt top, by adding sashing or setting strips between the blocks. Not all quilts made in blocks have sashing in between (see page 38), especially when the quilter wants to create a secondary design by arranging the blocks side by side, but the plain sashing in a

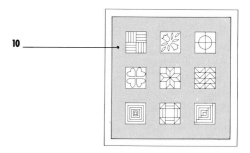

10 ⎯⎯⎯

10 Setting the blocks

neutral colour around the different designs of a sampler quilt sets all the blocks off very well and produces a sense of homogeneity.

The blocks are arranged in a pattern to give a pleasing balance of shades and colours across the quilt. If you have used different fabrics to make your blocks, lay them on the floor first to see whether you want to adjust the order of the blocks.

▲ *The quilt top begins to take shape; sashing or setting strips of unbleached calico divide the blocks.*

Choosing the sashing

The kind of sashing you decide on depends on the overall effect you want to create. For a quilt with a large number of similar blocks, a narrow sashing could look effective, perhaps blending in with the colours used in the blocks.

If you used mainly plain colours for the blocks, the sashing could be patterned for contrast. Or it could be a much darker, lighter or brighter colour to create the effect of a series of bars across the quilt.

1 *From fabric G, cut strips in the following measurements:*
six strips 22 cm (8¹/₂ in)×31.75 cm (12¹/₂ in)
four strips 22 cm (8¹/₂ in)×133.5 cm (52¹/₂ in)
two strips 22 cm (8¹/₂ in)×174 cm (68¹/₂ in)

2 *Taking 5 mm (¹/₄ in) seams each time, stitch one of the short strips between the Rail Fence block and the appliqué hearts block and another between the appliqué hearts block and the strip-pieced block.*

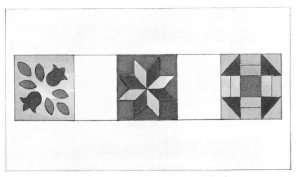

3 *In the same way, make a second row with the reverse appliqué block left, the Diamond Star in the middle and the Churn Dash block right.*

4 *Make a third row in the same way with the Sugar Bowl block left, the Flying Geese in the middle and the Log Cabin block right. Make sure that the Flying Geese fly up and down and that the dark edges of the Log Cabin are on the outside.*

5 *Stitch the four middle-length strips of calico to join the rows of blocks and to finish the outside edges of the rows. Make sure that you join the strips in the correct order, so that the Diamond Star is in the centre of the quilt top.*

6 *Add the two long strips of calico to the top and bottom of the quilt top.*

Adding a simple patchwork border to your quilt top is the final stage before you begin preparations for the quilting itself. This border uses a variation of the method that you used for the Strip-pieced block (see page 80), but on a much larger scale.

The squares in this border are 10 cm (4 in) wide, so their seams should line up with your block edges. As you attach the border, make

11

11 Adding a border

sure that the seam lines match; this will make the quilt top look very neat. You will need 72 squares to go around the edge, so you should be able to use the same repeat of the 6 fabrics 12 times. Keep them in the same order around the edges so that they don't distract the eye.

▶ *The completed quilt top: the patchwork border picks up the fabrics from the block designs.*

Detail of the sampler quilt border.

A
E
B
C
F
D

1 *From fabrics A, B, C, D, E and F, cut strips 11.5 cm (4½ in) wide. You will need a total length of about 150 cm (60 in) for each fabric, but this doesn't all have to be in one strip; if it works better with the fabric you have, you could make two pieced strips of 75 cm (30 in) each as you did for the strip-pieced block.*

2 *Use a 5 mm ($^1/_4$ in) seam to join the strips in the order A, E, B, C, F, D. This will give you a pieced strip (or two shorter ones) in which each individual strip is 10 cm (4 in) wide.*

3 *Using a rotary cutter (see page 44, Cutting fabrics), cut strips 11.5 cm ($4^1/_2$ in) wide across the width of the composite strip.*

4 *Join these new strips in groups of three to produce four strips containing 18 squares. Keep the squares in the same order each time.*

5 *Unpick the seam joining the final square (of fabric D) of two of the strips and join the extra squares to the beginnings of the other two strips, next to fabric A. This gives you two strips of 17 squares and two of 19.*

6 *Join one of the shorter strips to the top edge of the quilt top, taking a 5 mm ($^1/_4$ in) seam. Join the other short strip to the bottom edge, making sure that the colours are running in the same order around the quilt.*

7 *Join the longer strips to the edges of the quilt, making sure that the colours still run in the same order around the quilt. You are now ready to prepare for quilting.*

The piecing of your quilt top is now complete and it is time to mark the quilting patterns on to the fabric. It is best to do this before you tack the quilt top to the wadding; it is easier to make the marks accurately if you can rest the fabric on a hard surface. Once the wadding is in place, the surface becomes spongy. Two traditional patterns have been selected to quilt the sashing; a twisting cable repeat pattern and a

12

12 Marking the quilting patterns

SAMPLER QUILT

corner flower motif. The cable pattern has a 10 cm (4 in) repeat, so it fits in exactly three times along the edge of each block and exactly twice across the width of the sashing. The ends of the cables are finished off neatly by using the finishing templates.

A chess-board background texture has been chosen for the reverse appliqué block, so that you can practise stitching a texture of this kind. The checks need to be marked at this stage, too, but the other blocks don't need any marking as you will be using the seam lines as quilting guides.

There are many methods of marking quilt patterns (see page 48), but here we are using one of the easiest – tracing around a template with a water-soluble-ink pen. This gives you a good clear line to stitch on and, when you have finished, any visible marks can be gently sponged away with cold water.

There are, of course, many other designs which can be used on quilt tops; if you prefer to use alternative designs, there are plenty of ideas in the Pattern Libraries for quilted border patterns (see page 152), individual motifs (see page 134) and background textures (see page 154). Choose your design, scale it up or down to the appropriate size, then follow the instructions in this lesson for marking the designs onto the quilt top.

▲ *The marked quilt top: the lines made by the water-soluble-ink pen show up clearly on the fabrics.*

1 Make templates 12:1, 12:2, and 12:3 on page 71. Either use template plastic or cut them from paper and glue them onto card.

2 Start in the centre of each side and, working outwards, mark 11 repeats of template 12:1 down the centres of the sashing bands. Finish each end off neatly with template 12:2. Mark the two long pieces of sashing down the centre of the quilt in the same way.

3 On each short section of sashing, mark template 12:1 once and template 12:2 twice to create six mini-cables.

4 At each corner of the sashing, use template 12:3 to mark a flower motif.

5 On the reverse appliqué block, draw the diagonals across the block using a water-soluble-ink pen.

6 Working outwards from these lines in both directions, draw parallel lines 2.5 cm (1 in) apart; a quilter's ruler (see page 86) is very useful for this task. Draw the lines outside the appliqué shapes.

Now you are ready for the final stage, turning your quilt top into a quilt. Your fabric is marked with the quilting patterns and now needs to be put together with the wadding and the backing fabric.

All of the quilting can be worked by hand or by machine (see page 56, Quilting). If you quilt by machine, remember to finish off the threads neatly, ideally by pulling the top thread

13 ——————

13 Quilting the sampler quilt

through to the back of the quilt and knotting it with the bobbin thread. Or, if your sewing machine does a neat reverse stitch, you could work a few stitches in reverse at the end of each quilted line, but this shows on the right side unless you match the thread to the fabric colour exactly. Whether you are quilting by hand or machine, choose the colours of thread that you want to use for the quilting either to blend in or to stand out; we have used green on the calico, and pink and green on the blocks and border, but the patterns on the calico would also look effective quilted in pink or ecru.

▶ *The quilt top with all the quilting complete.*

1 *If your wadding is not already cut to the exact size, cut it to 200 cm (78 in) square. Cut a piece of calico the same size.*

2 *Following the instructions on page 52, make a sandwich of the calico, the wadding and the quilt top and secure the layers together with a grid of tacking. The calico and wadding should be 2 cm (³/₄ in) larger than the quilt top all around.*

3 Secure the quilt to the frame as shown on page 54. Unless you are using a full-size frame, work on one area of the quilt at a time, quilting from the centre out so that you minimize the risk of the fabric puckering. This applies to both hand and machine quilting.

4 Following the instructions on page 58 for quilting in the ditch, quilt the Flying Geese, Rail Fence, Log Cabin, Diamond Star, Strip-pieced and Churn Dash blocks. Quilt just outside the edges of the appliquéd Diamond Star shape.

5 Following the instructions on page 58 for outline quilting, quilt the Sugar Bowl block. Stitch inside the appliqué hearts in the same way and work a row of quilting stitches 5 cm ('/₄ in) outside the design as well.

6 Quilt the chess-board design around the reverse appliqué block, stitching a line 5 mm ('/₄ in) outside each leaf and flower and stopping each diagonal row on that line.

7 Quilt the cable designs first and then the corner motifs on the sashing.

8 Quilt the border squares either 'in the ditch' (see page 58) or 5 mm ('/₄ in) inside each patch. With a damp cloth, sponge away any blue marks remaining from the soluble-ink pen; your quilt is now almost finished.

You have now reached the final stage of your sampler quilt: binding the raw edges. There are many different ways of binding a quilt (see page 60) and the binding can be plain, patterned or pieced. Plain quilts are sometimes finished with shaped edges, such as scallops or rows of triangle shapes. Piped edges or frills, either single or double, can also look effective for some quilts. In this case, though, the

14 Binding the sampler quilt

SAMPLER QUILT

sampler quilt is quite ornate and an elaborate binding might have detracted from it, so we have chosen a simple binding worked in the same fabric that you used for the sashing and the backing. This gives a neat but unobtrusive finish. The squared corners are easier to work than mitred ones, but if you prefer the effect of mitred corners, as many quilters do, follow the instructions below.

Be sure to add your name and date to the quilt for posterity. You might even include the reason for making the quilt, for example, to celebrate a wedding or to remember a friend of many years. Embroider the data on the quilt top in the sashing or inside a block. Or, if your sewing machine can form letters, sew the details into the backing fabric before it is joined to the quilt top.

▲ *The finished quilt, with all the raw edges neatly concealed inside a calico binding.*

MITRED CORNERS

To mitre the corners of your binding, cut four strips 200 cm (78½ in) long, and join them in a large circle by making seams at each end as shown left. The tip of the seam should be 5 mm (¼ in) from the end of the strip and the angle should be an exact right angle. Trim the seams down each

side and cut away the tips, then press each length of binding in half lengthwise to mark the fold line. Attach the binding in the same way as for straight binding (see page 60), but machine stitch it all around the quilt edge before turning it to the back.

1 From the calico (fabric G), cut four strips 201×6.35 cm (79×2¹/₂ in). You will find it most accurate to use the rotary cutter and board for this; first cut a piece 201×25.4 cm (79×10 in), then cut this wide strip into four narrow ones.

2 Fold each of the strips in half lengthwise and press; this will give you a good fold line when you turn the strips over the quilt edges.

3 Open up one of the strips and place it face down on one side of the quilt, so that the raw edge aligns with the raw edge of the border (not the raw edge of the backing). Stitch a seam 5 mm (¹/₄ in) from the edge, by hand or machine. Repeat along the opposite quilt edge.

4 Fold the strips over the raw edges to the back of the quilt. Turn under 5 mm (¹/₄ in) and hem by hand to the calico backing to give a neat finish.

5 Trim the ends of the strips so that they align with the edges of the backing fabric.

6 Use the remaining two strips to bind the top and bottom of the quilt in the same way, tucking the raw ends in at the corners and stitching them in place.

4

Extending your skills

Wholecloth quilting is worked on one body of fabric. No piecing is involved and the decorative patterns are made entirely by the lines of quilting stitches rather than the patchwork designs.

Medallions are the main motifs used in wholecloth quilts. The medallion provides the main visual focus, usually forming a spectacular centrepiece. Some medallion designs have

Wholecloth cushion

histories and traditions. Heart shapes and lovers' knots, for instance, were traditionally stitched only on quilts meant for engaged or newlywed couples.

Many medallion designs were inspired by everyday objects – leaves, flowers, cords, fans, shells. Feather designs, in many different shapes, were especially popular. For this project, we have used a modern stylized flower shape which adds an attractive texture to the glazed cotton cushion cover.

MATERIALS

- Mid-blue cotton fabric: 1 circle, 50 cm (20 in) diameter; 2 rectangles, each 50×35.5 cm (20×14 in)
- Muslin or other backing fabric: 1 circle, 50 cm (20 in) diameter
- Thin, lightweight (2 oz) wadding: 1 circle, 50 cm (20 in) diameter
- Blue sewing thread (to match the cotton fabric)
- Blue quilting thread (darker than the cotton fabric)

14 in.

14 in.

▲ Chart for the Flower design.

1 Enlarge the chart for the flower to the correct size (see page 40). Remember to put in the centre dot. This will help you to position the design in the centre of the fabric.

2 Fold the blue circle in half, then in half again. Mark the centre point on the right side with a dot, using a fading-ink pen (see page 29).

3 Transfer the flower design to the right side of the blue cotton circle (see page 48), aligning the dot on the chart with the dot in the centre of the fabric.

4 Lay the muslin on a flat surface and and put the circle of batting on top, then the marked fabric, right side up. Baste together with a grid of horizontal and vertical stitches (see page 52).

5 Using the blue quilting thread, quilt the design (see page 56). Begin in the centre and work outwards to prevent puckering. When your quilting is complete, remove the tacking.

6 Press and stitch a small double seam on one long edge of each rectangle.

7 Place the rectangles face up on a flat surface. Place the quilted medallion face down on top so that the seamed edges overlap and the sides are level with the edges of the circle. Tack around 2.5 cm (1 in) from edges.

8 Stitch around the edge twice by machine for strength. Remove the tacking. Trim the seam to 5 mm (¹/₄ in); trim the excess fabric from the cushion back. Be careful not to cut through the seam line. Clip seam.

9 Turn the cushion cover right side out and press the backs carefully. Don't press the quilted areas. If the front of the cover is creased, hold a hot steam iron a few centimetres above the quilting for a few seconds.

The Amish people follow a simple and industrious way of life. Their stress on simplicity is noticeable in the plain, sometimes stark beauty of their quilts. Many Amish quilts are made from hand-dyed cottons in bright colours; black pieces are added, giving more intensity to the surrounding colours. The Amish sometimes use block patterns, but more usually a large central design is surrounded by

Amish lap quilt

one or two borders; quilting with contrasting threads shows off the exquisite patterns in the stitches. The colours used in the oldest Amish quilts, from Pennsylvania, are usually in the cool part of the spectrum. We have used these colours in this simple patchwork design called, among other things, Roman Stripes.

MATERIALS

- Cotton fabric:
  0.25 m×152.4 cm (¼ yd×60 in)
  of each of 6 colours – pale pink,
  dark pink, mauve, purple, pale
  blue, dark blue
- Black cotton fabric:
  1.4 m×152.4 cm
  (1½ yd×60 in); 2×3 m (6 ft
  2 in×4 ft 2 in).
- Thin wadding: 1.8×1.2 m
  (6×4 ft).
- Muslin: 1.8×1.2 m
  (6×4 ft).
- Matching sewing thread
- Right-angle triangle template
  with shorter sides of 12 in.

1 Use a rotary cutter to cut the coloured cotton fabric lengthwise into 5 cm (2 in) strips (see page 44).

2 Stitch the strips of fabric together along the long edges to make four wide strips. Work in this order each time – purple, light pink, dark blue, mauve, dark pink, light blue. Use 5 mm (¼ in) seam allowance.

3 Position the template so that the 90° point is on one edge of one wide strip and the long edge is along the other. Use a rotary cutter to cut a triangle from the strip-pieced fabric. Turn the template round and cut another triangle. Continue in this way until you have cut 24 triangles, 12 in each direction.

4 Use the same template to cut 24 triangles from the black fabric. Place the short sides of the template along the grain. With right sides together, join the long edge of a black triangle to the long edge of a strip-pieced triangle. Repeat to form 24 blocks.

5 If necessary, trim the blocks slightly to square them up. Follow the layout shown in the photograph to join the blocks in four rows of six, then join the rows together to form the quilt top.

6 Layer the muslin, the wadding and the quilt top (see page 52). Tack the layers together. Stitch by hand or machine along the seam lines between the blocks and between the triangles. Remove the tacking.

7 Place the quilted patchwork on the backing fabric, wrong sides together. Turn over each edge of backing fabric 5 mm (¼ in), then 5 mm (¼ in) again. Tack backing over the edges of the patchwork; slipstitch into place. Remove tacking.

E nglish patchwork is pieced work that is produced by stitching together pieces of fabric that have been tacked on to paper shapes. It is very time-consuming, so is not the best method for traditional block patterns which can be stitched far more quickly by the conventional method. It is, however, very useful for shapes which cannot easily be joined with long straight seams, such as hexagons, diamond

English patchwork

stars, octagons and patterns such as Tumbling Blocks or Baby's Blocks (see page 125).

To assemble the pieces for English patchwork, cut the shapes from paper, such as typing paper, then cut corresponding fabric shapes, with a 5 mm (¼ in) seam allowance all round. The fabric is then tacked over the paper, turning the raw edges to the back and the shapes are oversewn together to build up the pattern. Here, the paper shapes are left in place to stiffen the decoration, but normally they are removed when the tacking is taken out.

For an eye-catching variation, sew six hexagons instead of seven and make a wreath decoration by leaving out the middle shape.

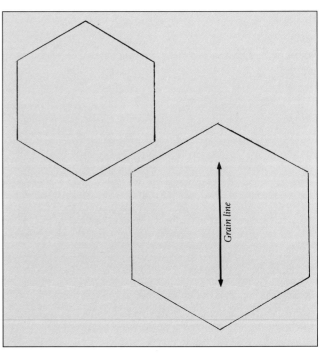

▲ Template A for the paper shapes.

▲ Template B for the fabric shapes.

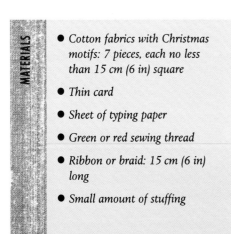

MATERIALS

- Cotton fabrics with Christmas motifs: 7 pieces, each no less than 15 cm (6 in) square
- Thin card
- Sheet of typing paper
- Green or red sewing thread
- Ribbon or braid: 15 cm (6 in) long
- Small amount of stuffing

1 Trace the templates onto thin card, and cut them out very accurately. Mark the grain line onto template B. Cut two shapes from each fabric using template B. Using template A, cut 14 paper shapes.

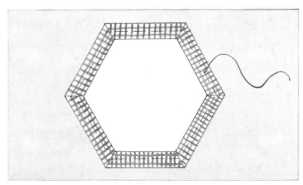

2 Tack each piece of fabric to a paper shape, stitching down the 5 mm (¼ in) overlap all round. Tie a knot in the end of your tacking thread and start stitching with the knot on the right side; this will make it easier to remove the tacking.

3 When all your shapes are tacked, take two hexagons of different fabrics and place them right sides together. Stitch them together along one side, oversewing with close, firm stitches. Start and finish the thread securely.

4 Continue joining hexagons to form a rosette of six different hexagons around a central one; make sure that all the seams between them are stitched. Join the other hexagons in the same way to form a mirror-image rosette.

5 Place the rosettes, paper sides together, with the same fabric hexagons backing each other at the top, and blind-stitch around the edges of the rosettes. Stitch the ends of the hanging loop into the seam at each side of the top hexagon and leave two or three sides open for stuffing.

6 Pad the shape gently with a small amount of the stuffing and close up the final edges of the rosette. Don't over-stuff or the shape of the decoration will be distorted. Remove the tacking.

This striking patchwork is a type of appliqué. The patches of fabric are laid onto a background and the raw edges are covered with a length of binding. The final result resembles a stained glass window; the binding makes lines between the fabric pieces in the same way that leading separates panes of coloured glass.

If all the lines in the patchwork design are straight, any kind of binding can be used for

Stained glass wallhanging

the 'leading'. If any of the lines are curved, you will need to use bias binding so that the tape can be shaped to follow the curves. You can use bought bias binding or cut strips of fabric on the bias; the latter is useful when you want a particular colour or size of bias binding.

This project uses the traditional black binding over bright, jewel-coloured fabrics.

MATERIALS

- Pale green cotton fabric: 75 cm (30 in) square
- Calico (or other backing fabric): 75 cm (30 in) square
- Thin wadding: 75 cm (30 in) square
- Bright pink cotton fabric: 45 cm (18 in) square
- Bright purple cotton fabric: 45 cm (18 in) square
- Bright jade green cotton fabric: 35 cm (14 in) square
- Medium jade green cotton fabric: 35 cm (14 in) square
- 2.5 cm (1 in) wide black bias binding: 14.75m (16 yd)
- Black cotton sewing thread

▲ *Chart for flowers and leaves.*　**76cm (30 in)**

76 cm (30 in)

1 Enlarge the chart to the correct size (see page 40). Go over it with dark felt-tip pen and trace it onto the right side of the pale green fabric. The lines will be covered by the bias binding.

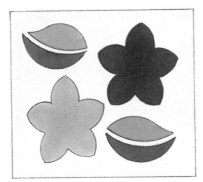

2 Use the enlarged drawing to cut templates for the flower and leaf shapes. Cut one flower from each of the purple and pink fabrics and two half-leaves from the two green fabrics.

3 Lay out the fabric pieces in the correct position on the pale green fabric. Tack them into place.

4 Pin and tack pieces of bias binding, with the edges folded under, along all the lines of the design. Make sure that raw ends are covered by the next piece of binding.

5 Lay the wadding on top of the backing fabric and lay the flower design, face up, on top. Tack the layers together with a grid of vertical and horizontal stitches (see page 52).

6 Machine stitch along both edges of each strip of bias binding. Stitch the inside edge of each curve first; this prevents the binding stretching out of shape.

7 Remove tacking. Add a small circle of black fabric to the centre of the flower to cover the raw ends of bias binding. Turn under and hand stitch.

8 Bind the raw edges of the square with more black bias binding.

9 Attach tape loops or a casing made from bias binding to the back of the project to hang it up.

Cathedral window patchwork is an unusual technique. It is neither pieced, appliquéd nor quilted. It requires no wadding as the thickness comes from folding squares of fabric over on themselves. The finished result is rather three-dimensional in effect, with an overall design which is highly textured.

The base squares are usually made in plain colours, with the 'windows' cut from prints.

EXTENDING YOUR SKILLS

Cathedral window

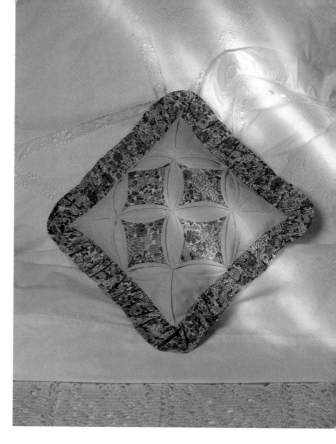

Interesting effects can be achieved by reversing this idea; use a small print for the frames and either a plain colour, a large print or a single motif in the windows. The shape and size of the panels lend themselves perfectly to this herb cushion design and provide an easy introduction to this technique. The pot pourri or scented herbs will gradually release their fragrance into a room or drawer.

MATERIALS

- Pink cotton fabric: 4 squares, each 26.5 cm (10 in)
- Pink printed cotton fabric: 0.5 m (½ yd)
- Pink sewing thread to match
- Pot pourri or scented herbs to stuff cushion

1 Fold one square in half, wrong sides together, and stitch a 5 mm (¼ in) seam along both short edges. Repeat the process for the other squares.

2 On each square, pin together the tops of the seams and then pin the remaining raw edges together along the top. Leaving an opening for turning, stitch a 5 mm (¼ in) seam.

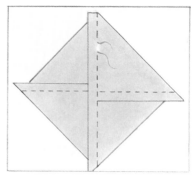

3 Clip the excess fabric diagonally at each of the corners. This will make the shapes lie flat after they are turned right side out.

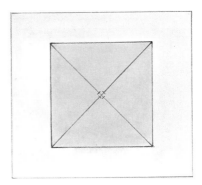

4 Turn the seamed squares to the right side. Use the tip of a bodkin to push out the corners. Press into square shapes. The opening will be hidden when the cushion is finished.

5 Lay one square flat with the seams on top, then bring all four corners to the centre. Press firmly. Repeat for the remaining squares.

6 Catch the corners of each square down at the centre with very small stitches through to the back.

7 Put two squares together so that the folded sides are facing each other; oversew down one side. Repeat for the other pair of squares, then stitch the pairs together in the same way.

8 Cut four squares of printed fabric a little smaller than the square made by points A, B, C and D. Pin them inside the lines made by the folds on each side of the shape.

9 Roll the edges of the 'windows' over the edges of the printed fabric squares. Stitch the edges down, catching the corners together with two small stitches. Roll and catch down the edges just outside the windows.

10 From the printed fabric, cut a length 8.25 cm (3¼ in) × the complete width. Fold it lengthways and press fold. Run a gathering thread along the bottom, 5 mm (¼ in) in from the raw edges, and pull to make a frill.

11 Cut a square of printed fabric the same size as your patchwork square plus 5 mm (¼ in) all round. Pin the frill to the cushion top, right sides together. Stitch with a 5 mm (¼ in) seam all round, then press frill out.

12 Place the patchwork square on the printed backing square, wrong sides together. Slipstitch three edges, then stuff gently with pot pourri. Slipstitch the final edge closed.

F olded patchwork has several variations. The technique used here is also called Somerset patchwork and can be used for items like cushions, cards and wallhangings. Folded patchwork of this kind is not suitable for bed quilts, however, as there are raw edges inside the folds which would tend to fray with frequent washing. Another folded technique, Prairie Points, is constructed so that the raw edges are

EXTENDING YOUR
SKILLS

Folded star

sealed; because of this extra protection, it is particularly recommended for items that have to be washed.

This project uses two patterned fabrics in Christmas colours. The circles are arranged so that a red star appears in the design. If you fold your fabric so that the same motif shows each time, you can create a secondary pattern within the star. Use unusual fabrics to vary the design.

For appliqué shapes with extra dimension, use small pieces of folded patchwork to make trees or flowers; bind the edges and attach to a background. This patchwork is usually constructed from the centre out, but for flowers and trees you can begin at the outside.

MATERIALS

- Calico, or other foundation fabric: 13×13 cm (5×5 in)
- Red Christmas printed cotton fabric: 11.5 cm (⅛ yd)
- Green Christmas printed fabric: 11.5 cm (⅛ yd)
- Matching sewing thread
- Glue
- Greetings card mount with round opening approximately 9.5 cm (3¾ in) diameter
- Red frame, approximately 11.5 cm (4½ in) square

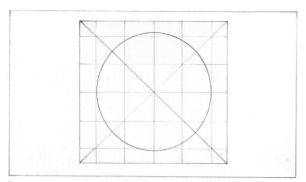

1 On the square of foundation fabric, draw in diagonals from corner to corner. From the centre outwards, draw a grid of 2.5 cm (1 in) squares – a quilter's ruler (see page 28) is useful for drawing parallel lines. In the centre of the grid, draw a circle the same size as the one on the card.

2 From the red fabric cut 12 rectangles each measuring 3.8×6.4 cm (1½×2½ in). From the green fabric, cut 16 rectangles the same size. For accuracy and speed, use a rotary cutter (see page 45).

3 Fold and press under 5 mm (¹/₄ in) along one long edge of each one of the rectangles.

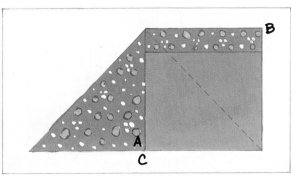

4 Fold and press points A and B to point C on all pieces, placing wrong sides together as shown. You now have 28 folded triangles; 12 red and 16 green. All show the right side of the fabric on both sides.

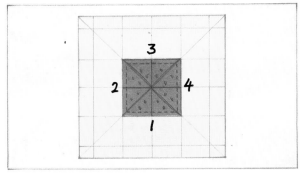

5 Lay 4 red triangles down on the centre of the foundation square, folds up as shown. Use the guidelines to help you position them accurately. Secure each point with an invisible stitch; stitch to the foundation with running stitches around the edges.

6 Lay 4 green triangles, points in, over the first 4 red ones. Overlap evenly all round, but position the green triangles further out than the red row. Use running stitches round the long edges as before . Work another row of 4 green triangles in the same way.

7 Now add a row of 8 red triangles, positioned in alternating layers as before. Finish off with a row of 8 green triangles to complete the star.

8 Tack, then stitch just outside the circle on the foundation fabric and cut out the completed circle and star. Glue around the edges of the star shape. Place the star behind the opening in the card, making sure that it is accurately centred. Place in frame.

Trapunto quilting, like conventional quilting, uses a layer of wadding, but in trapunto only certain areas are padded rather than the whole of the item. The top layer of fabric is tacked to a firm backing layer, then the chosen areas are stitched to form hollow pockets. These are then lightly stuffed, producing an intriguing three-dimensional effect.

The project here uses a fabric-painted

Trapunto table mat

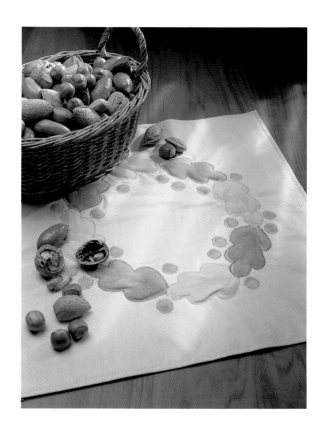

design, but you could just as easily use a printed fabric or one of the specially printed panels. Work the stitching by hand or by machine; machine stitching is much quicker if you have large areas to cover. If you stitch by hand, use a firm backstitch in a strong thread so that the stitching gives a definite outline to the pockets.

- Pale yellow cotton fabric: 45 cm (18 in) square
- Calico or other backing fabric: 2 squares, each 45×45 cm (18×18 in)
- Fabric paints: medium and dark yellow; medium and dark orange; medium and dark moss green. (You can purchase colours separately or mix your own.)
- Brushes
- Yellow sewing thread (to match yellow fabric)
- Stuffing

▲ Actual size chart for the table mat design.

1 Draw a circle 14 cm (5¹/₂ in) in diameter and arrange leaf and berry shapes around it. Go over the design lines with black felt-tip pen.

2 Place the yellow fabric, right side up, over the design and trace the main lines using a matching crayon or silverpoint (see page 49).

3 Use the yellow, green and orange fabric paints to colour in the leaves and berries; alternate yellow leaves and green leaves.

4 With slightly darker shades of the same colours, add veins to the leaves and details to berries. When the paint is dry, set the colours according to the manufacturer's directions.

5 Place the painted panel over one square of the backing fabric, wrong sides together, matching edges. Tack with a grid of horizontal and vertical stitches (see page 52).

6 Outline the leaves and berries with machine zigzag or straight stitch; use back stitches if stitching by hand.

7 Behind each pocket formed by the stitched outline, cut a small 1.25 to 2 cm (¹/₂ to ³/₄ in) long slit in the backing fabric. Be very careful not to cut through the top fabric.

8 Use a small amount of stuffing to pad each stitched pocket, checking your progress from the front. Don't over-stuff or the fabric will distort. Close the slits in the backing fabric with small oversewing stitches.

9 Tack the second square of backing fabric to the back of the mat, wrong sides together. Fold raw edges to the inside; close with two rows of topstitching around outside edges.

Italian, or corded, quilting involves stitching two layers of fabric together in a decorative pattern of lines and channels. When the stitching is complete, the channels are threaded with cord or thick wool. This raises the top fabric and produces a textured pattern. Italian quilting is excellent for strong linear designs like this Celtic knot, worked on silk for a skirt pocket. The stitching and quilting are completed

Corded pocket

before the pocket is attached to the garment. (For a ready-made garment, remove the pocket to embellish it, then stitch in place again.) This design is worked on a pocket for an evening skirt, but would also work made smaller to decorate a shirt pocket.

MATERIALS

- Silk fabric: about 5 cm (2 in) larger all round than pocket pattern piece
- Firmly woven silk fabric for backing: same size as above
- Fine cotton cord: 1.8 m (2 yd)
- Cotton or silk thread to match silk fabric
- Large-eyed tapestry needle

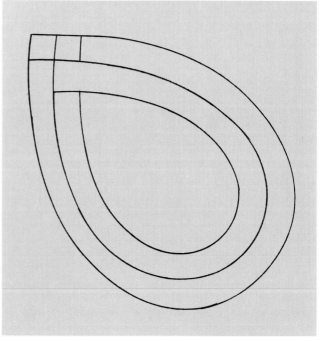

▲ One quarter of the Celtic Knot pattern, actual size for tracing.

1 Trace each quarter of the pattern (opposite below) on the same piece of paper. Turn the paper and reposition it carefully for each quarter.

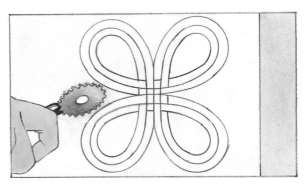

2 Transfer the design to the right side of the silk fabric, using the tracing or prick and pounce method (see page 49). Allow at least 2.5 cm (1 in) margin of plain fabric around the outside edge of the design.

3 Place the silk on top of the backing fabric, wrong sides together. Tack together with a grid of horizontal and vertical stitches (see page 53).

4 Using back stitches and three strands of cotton or silk thread, stitch along all the lines of the design to form channels. When the stitching is complete, press the design with a warm steam iron.

5 Thread the tapestry needle with a length of cord. Take the needle through the backing fabric at the beginning of one channel. Thread all the channels with cord, taking the needle out of the backing fabric at the end of each channel. Along tight curves, you may need to take the needle in and out of backing fabric several times.

6 When the design is completely corded, lay it face down on a soft cloth and press it on the wrong side with a warm steam iron. Centre the pocket pattern over the design, cut out, and continue making the garment.

Sashiko quilting is a traditional Japanese technique. The stitching is worked in bold threads; the thickness depends on the thickness of the fabric. The stitches are longer than for ordinary quilting. Stitch length for Sashiko is about twice as long on the front as on the back. The designs are usually geometric repeats. This silk evening bag illustrates the use of several different designs inside straight

Sashiko bag

outlines. Sashiko work can be flat or padded; this project is gently padded with a thin layer of wadding to give it extra texture.

Because the stitches are designed to show, it is important to make them look as even and attractive as possible. On straight lines, pick up as many stitches as possible on your needle so that you get into an even rocking rhythm; on curves it will only be practical to pick up one or two stitches to keep the curve smooth. Try to sew the same number of stitches per couple of centimetres throughout the design and make sure that they don't overlap.

MATERIALS

- Jade green silk fabric: two pieces, 54.5×19 cm (21½×7½ in) each; 9×12.5 cm (3½×5 in) rectangle; 7.5×7.5 cm (3×3 in) square

- Thin (2oz) polyester or silk wadding: 53.5×17.75 cm (21×7 in)

- Iron-on interfacing (light)

- Gold thread

- Small gold beads

- Green silk thread to match

- Green sewing thread to match

- Thin gold or jade cord

- Thick jade cord for handle

1 *Enlarge the chart to the correct size (see page 40). Using a crayon slightly darker than the silk or a silverpoint (see page 49), transfer the design onto the right side of one of the large pieces of silk.*

118

2 *Place the silk pieces right sides together and pin the wadding in the centre of the top piece. Machine stitch round the rectangle, leaving one short side open for turning. Clip across the corners and remove the pins.*

3 *Turn right side out and slipstitch the open end, turning under 5 mm (¹⁄₄ in) of each piece of fabric to make a rectangle 17.75×53.5 cm (7×21 in)*

4 *Tack the layers together with a grid of horizontal and vertical stitches (see page 52). Using the gold thread, make Sashiko running stitches along all the lines of the design. Begin each thread with a small knot pulled into the lining.*

▲ *Chart for the evening bag.*

16.5 cm (6¹⁄₂ in)

49.5 cm (19¹⁄₂ in)

Back of sashiko bag.

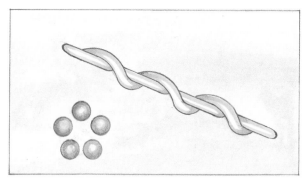

5 Using the gold thread, whip a line of stitches through the running stitches that divide each pattern block; this gives a solid gold line. Add several gold beads where indicated on the chart.

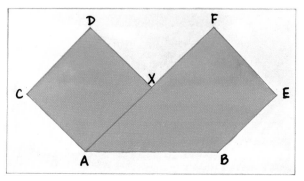

6 Lay the quilted rectangle face down; fold along line AB to make the shape shown.

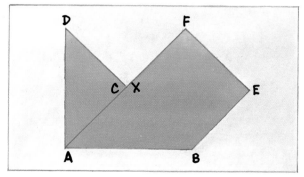

7 Fold corner C to point X; turn the piece over. Fold corner E to point X. Pin the edges together where they meet so that the bag keeps its shape.

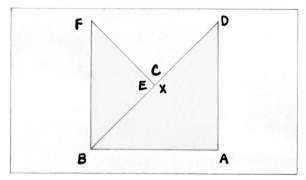

8 Turn the bag inside out and slipstitch from corner A to point CX and from corner B to point EX.

9 Add iron-on interfacing to back of two small green silk pieces. Fold the rectangular piece in half across its width, right sides together, and sew together with a 5 mm (¼ in) seam allowance. Clip the corners and turn right side out. Slipstitch the open ends closed to make a 5 cm (2½ in) square.

120

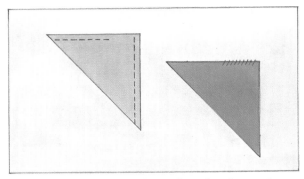

10 Fold the square of silk diagonally, right sides together, and stitch 5 mm (¹/₄ in) seams along two sides, leaving a small opening for turning. Clip corners, turn right side out and slipstitch the opening closed.

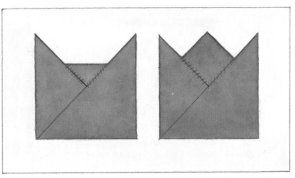

11 Slipstitch the triangular piece into the V shape at the front of the bag and the square piece into the V at the back, working the stitches neatly from the inside of the bag.

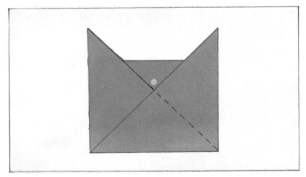

12 Fold the top half of the square over the front of the bag and add a popper or other closure underneath the flap.

13 Cut a length of thick cord for the handle; stitch the raw ends invisibly to the points of the bag sides. If the cord is bulky, wrap the end in the point of the bag, then stitch the diagonal sides together to hide it.

14 Add thin cord to the seam lines on the front and back of the bag, using invisible slipstitches.

15 Make three tassels from the gold thread and the green thread; stitch them to the bottom corners of the bag and the tip of the front flap.

5
Pattern library

This section shows many popular piecing and quilting patterns, both traditional and modern. The Pattern Library is divided into types of patterns to make it easy to use. For example, nine-patch block designs are all together, as are Log Cabin designs, quilted motifs, pieced borders, block and sashing combinations and so on.

You can use the patterns here in several ways. You might want to choose an alternative design for one of the sections in the sampler quilt. Or incorporate the designs here into projects found elsewhere. Or you can use the designs for your own projects. Mix and match the patterns to create your own unique designs.

Top: Fans variation block

Right: Strip-pieced quilt and border

Left: Sunflower Star

Bottom left: Star Blocks with Sawtooth border

Below: Tumbling Blocks with Baby Blocks

Four-patch blocks

Four-patch block designs range from very simple patterns to very complex ones. In some designs, such as Attic Windows *and* Oh Susannah, *all of the quarters in the block are identical; each quarter is stitched in the same relationship to the centre of the block. Some designs, such as* King's X, *use quarters made as mirror images; others, such as* Double Four Patch, *use two quarters made up in one arrangement and two in another.*

Simple Four Patch

Double Four Patch

Rail Fence

Attic Windows

Four patch with pinwheels and wholecloth

Pinwheel

Oh Susannah

Pinwheel variation

Nine Patch in Four Patch

Flyfoot

Double 2

Sawtoothed Square

Sawtooth

Star

Eight Star Flower

King's X

Nine-patch blocks

Because nine-patch blocks use more pieces, the possibilities for design variations are greater and you can create some very complex effects. Nine-patch blocks are rarely made with each patch identical. In some designs, such as **Rolling Stone** and **Corner Nine Patch**, *the middle patch is a plain square of fabric. In the* **Nine-Patch Variation**, *the middle patch is pieced so that it provides a visual focus for the block.* Many nine-patch designs build up a complex pattern across the patches, such as **Jacob's Ladder**. **Maple Leaf** *is another example of a simple picture built from regular patches.*

Basic Nine Patch

Nine Patch variation

Corner Nine Patch

Bear's Paw

Basic nine-patch blocks with wholecloth blocks

Ohio Star

Star variation

54 or 40, or Fight

Jacob's Ladder

Cross and Crown

Maple Leaf

Card Trick

Churn Dash

Rolling Stone

Irregular blocks

Irregular blocks are less straightforward to piece. Some require curved seams or set-in seams, such as **Covered Bridge** *and* **Fruit Basket**. *In others, the piecing is all in straight seams, but the patches are quite complex; for example,* **Pine Tree**, **Pieced Tulip** *and* **School House**. *If you are making one of these blocks, look carefully at the piecing required. Break down the design into its component patches and try to do most of the piecing in straight seams.*

Many of the irregular block designs use a combination of piecing and appliqué. **Grandmother's Fan**, **Dresden Plate** *and their variations – some of the most popular block designs – are pieced first, then appliquéd onto a background square. The* **Carolina Lily** *design is pieced in patches, but the fine stems are then appliquéd onto the block (see page 78). These designs still make square blocks when they are finished, so they can be substituted for any of the blocks in the sampler quilt or any project that calls for a block design.*

Attic Windows

Attic Windows variation

Four Crown

Sailboat

School House

Covered Bridge

Pieced Tulip

Carolina Lily

Grandmother's Fan variation

Fruit Basket

Tree of Life

Pine Tree

Dresden Plate

Grandmother's Fan

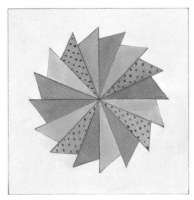

Dresden Plate variation

Non-block designs

The pieced designs on these pages create fascinating shapes which can be used for whole quilts or appliquéd to a plain background. Spectacular star shapes, such as **Lone Star** *and* **Broken Star** *can be built from the 45° diamond shapes shown. 60° diamonds can be used to piece hexagons. If you make partial star or hexagon motifs from triangles, the quilt can then be pieced in strips and the strips joined by machine, an easier approach than the traditional English patchwork method (see page 106). Triangles can also be used to build up large pieced areas.* **1000 Pyramids** *use 65° triangles.*

Template for Lone Star

Lone Star

Template for 1000 Pyramids

1000 Pyramids

Central non-block design with Flying Geese border

Hexagon Ferris Wheel

Tumbler

Tumbling Blocks

Star variation

Broken Star

Giant Dahlia

Complex Double Wedding Ring

Flying Geese

Appliqué designs

The shapes in appliqué are stitched onto the fabric and can be as simple or complex as you like. There is an unlimited number of designs that can be used for appliqué; these pages show some of the popular ones. If you are new to appliqué, try simple shapes first, such as leaves, flowers and birds. Follow the guidelines on page 78 for turning under the raw edges and stitching the shapes to the background. Once you become more confident, you can begin to use more sophisticated designs. Try the **Rose of Sharon** *patterns,* **Crossed Tulip** *or* **Radical Rose***. Appliqué shapes can be used on blocks (see Sampler quilt, page 78), or they can be arranged on a much larger background. Appliqué also works well on a background shape, such as a circle, heart or trefoil.*

Making your own appliqué designs is quite easy. Choose simple shapes or smooth out the lines of more complicated ones; avoid very sharp points and very fine lines. Draw your design full size, then follow the instructions on page 42 for producing templates.

Leaf

Dove

Flower

Shamrock

Rose wreath appliquéd quilt

Tulip detail

Bird

Tulip

Pear

Radical Rose

Oak Leaf

Ohio Rose

Rose of Sharon

Rose of Sharon variation

Crossed Tulip

Log Cabin blocks

The traditional **Log Cabin** block was used in the sampler quilt (see page 80), but the technique has many other variations. Two strips of fabric used in each layer produce a chevron design. **Court House Steps** applies the strips of fabric on opposite sides before completing the square with the remaining two strips. This design is often made with light and dark fabrics. The basic design can be varied further: make four smaller blocks to build up into a **Log Cabin** four-patch; make the fabrics different widths to produce an off-centre design; stitch the strips at a slant; stitch the strips round a central rectangle rather than a square.

The **Log Cabin** technique can be used to build up blocks of different shapes, too. Work in the same way, but begin with a triangle or a diamond.

Basic Log Cabin

Log Cabin variation

White House Steps

Log Cabin four-patch

Basic Log Cabin

Thick and thin Log Cabin

Rectangular Log Cabin

Log Cabin corner

Pineapple

Log Cabin Court House Steps

Triangle Log Cabin

Diamond Log Cabin

Crazy Log Cabin

Log Cabin combinations

All of the designs on these pages are made from different types of **Log Cabin** *blocks. Using the traditional division of light and dark fabrics, several identical* **Log Cabin** *blocks can be stitched together to make secondary patterns, many of which have their own names, like* **Straight Furrows** *and* **Barn Raising***. The blocks can be combined so that the light or dark squares form pinwheels, using triangles, squares, rectangles or parallelograms. Off-centre* **Log Cabin** *blocks combine to make pretty star shapes, while several* **Pineapple** *blocks together create a design of secondary circles.*

Log Cabin Star

Pineapple Log Cabin design

Block for Log Cabin Star

Off-centre narrow logs block

Off-centre narrow logs combination

Off-centre wide logs

Log Cabin Cross

Pineapple

Straight Furrow

Barn Raising

Log Cabin variation

Strip-piecing patterns

The basic principle of strip-piecing involves joining strips of several fabrics, then cutting the new fabric into strips or other shapes and reassembling them to create a secondary pattern. This principle can be applied to create many different patterns, even using a basic combination of two fabric strips. Strips can be cut into diamonds or triangles and reassembled into stars and hexagons, which can in turn be built into larger patterns if you wish.

If you join many strips of fabric, you can create very complex designs like bargello patterns. Irish Chain *consists of strip-pieced blocks (each made up of five strips of five squares in alternating colours) alternated with plain blocks that have been appliquéd or strip-pieced with a contrasting square in each corner.*

Sew together horizontal strips of even widths. Cut into vertical strips as indicated above.

Cut into strips. Each new strip will contain several pieces of joined fabric.

Strip-pieced Irish Chain

Reassemble the new strips so that there are diagonal lines of identical fabrics.

Sew together two strips of equal width. Cut the strip-pieced fabrics into different shapes. A 45° triangle will make patterns 1 and 2; 90° triangles will make pattern 3, and squares will make pattern 4.

Strip-piecing pattern 1

Strip-piecing pattern 2

Strip-piecing pattern 3

Strip-piecing pattern 4

Sew together three strips of even widths and cut into 60° triangles. These triangles can be reassembled to create unusual hexagon designs.

Hexagon

Hexagon variation

Seminole patterns

Seminole work is a variation of strip piecing, but is usually stitched to create long borders to be inserted into garments, bags, quilt borders and such. Strips of fabric are joined in the normal way, then cut either straight or at an angle to form smaller strips. These smaller strips are then laid at an angle or offset or turned top to bottom and joined once again. Any excess fabric is cut off. Using this method you can create chevrons, zigzags, diamonds, chess-board designs and many other variations.

Accuracy is very important in Seminole patchwork. A rotary cutter is excellent for this work. The original strips must be cut and joined accurately; cut any angled strips very carefully so that they are all at exactly the same angle. When rejoined, they need to be positioned against each other carefully so that each part is identical.

Sew together strips of various widths. Cut at an angle.

Reposition the cut strips at an opposite slant and reassemble to create different effects.

This sawtooth pattern is formed from diamond sections cut from two strip-pieced fabrics. The cut sections are turned and joined at an angle, then trimmed.

The two strip-pieced sections above and below are cut at opposite angles and joined to form a chevron pattern (right).

Chevron combination

143

Block and sashing combinations

Blocks are separated with lines of sashing or setting strips (see page 38). These act as frames for the blocks, so that each design can be seen and appreciated in isolation as well as forming part of the whole design.

There are many different ways of setting blocks and some of the methods are shown here. Blocks can be joined in shapes or in strips of several blocks, with each group then separated from the others by sashing. Amish quilters (see page 104) often set one or more blocks 'on point' or as diamonds.

If the blocks are complex, sashing generally looks best in plain or lightly patterned fabrics. Some sashing designs use two different fabrics. Other designs look like criss-cross strips; the square where two strips intersect uses a different fabric, different colour, or even a small pieced block.

Diamond blocks

Nine-patch blocks

Star blocks

Plain sashing with double border

Maple Leaf blocks

Nine-patch variation

On point sashing

Churn Dash blocks

Plain sashing

Cross sashing

Pieced-block sashing

Octagonal design

Strip-pieced sashing

Churn Dash variation in border

Alternate blocks in border

Combining blocks

Quilters like to make use of the secondary patterns formed when blocks are sewn together without sashing. When certain block designs are placed edge to edge, the lines of one block carry visually into the next.

Some blocks can be used to create different patterns: **Sugar Bowl** *(see page 76) can also make the meandering* **Drunkard's Path** *and the* **Love Ring** *flower. New outlines appear from parts of several blocks put together: each leaf of the* **Ozark Maple Leaf** *pattern is made from a large part of one block and small triangles on adjoining blocks. (Continued on page 148)*

Sugar Bowl basic block 1

Sugar Bowl basic block 2

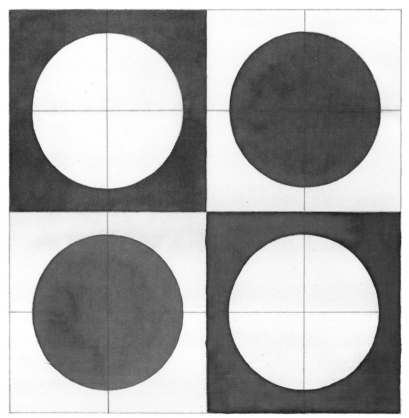

Sugar Bowl basic blocks 1 and 2 combined

Love Ring

Drunkard's Path

Maple Leaf basic block, light

Ozark Maple Leaf

Maple Leaf basic block, dark

Maple Leaf combined variation

◁ *Familiar block patterns can be adapted to form new patterns. The pattern at bottom right was created by alternating* **Rolling Stone** *blocks with an adaptation.*

Snail Trail *makes a continuous pattern across the quilt by alternating pattern blocks of light or dark.*

Snail Trail component block

Snail Trail

Snail Trail component block

Snail Trail combined

Flyfoot block

Flyfoot combined with reverse color blocks

Windmill block

Windmill adapted and combined

Rolling Stone block

Rolling Stone adapted block

Rolling Stone combined

Pattern library

Pieced border patterns

When planning your border pattern, try to use a motif or an idea from your main quilt. If your central patchwork has a strong pattern of stars or squares, then choose a border pattern based on stars or squares. Sawtooth borders are good for blocks featuring many triangles, such as Bear's Paw, Basket *and* Tree of Life; *borders using curves are good for edging quilts with curved seams in the blocks, such as* Drunkard's Path. *Strip-pieced borders with quarter-circle corners look just right on* Dresden Plate *or* Grandmother's Fan *quilts, while diamond borders make spectacular edgings for complex star designs.*

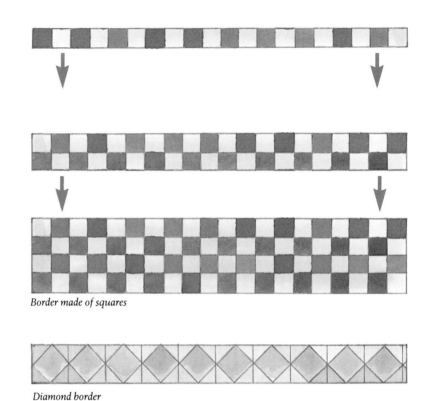

Border made of squares

Diamond border

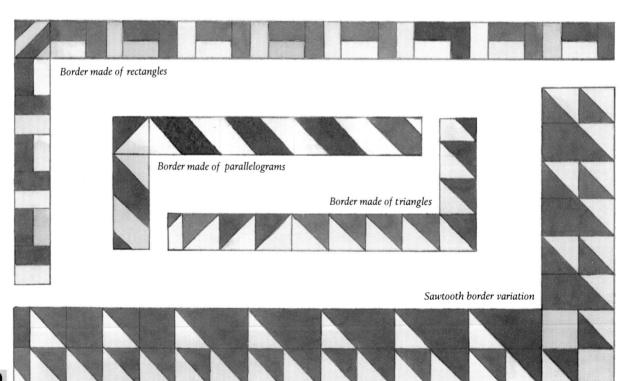

Border made of rectangles

Border made of parallelograms

Border made of triangles

Sawtooth border variation

150

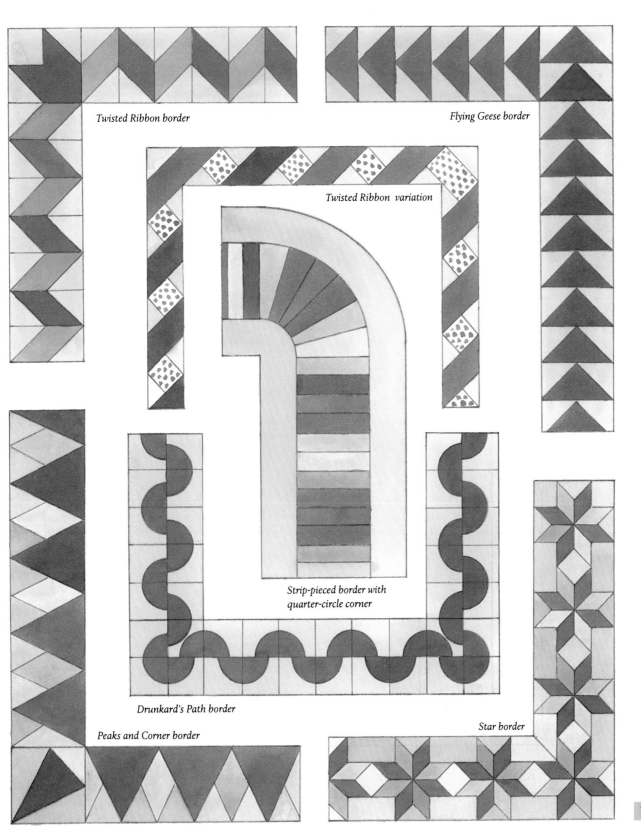

Twisted Ribbon border

Flying Geese border

Twisted Ribbon variation

Strip-pieced border with
quarter-circle corner

Drunkard's Path border

Peaks and Corner border

Star border

Quilted border patterns

Border patterns for quilting are numerous and varied. Like the medallions, many of the traditional border patterns use everyday shapes such as flowers, stars and feathers. Many designs have evolved using variations of plaits (three or more strands), twisted cables and waves. Complex border designs often combine several elements, such as a double cable twist of feathers with flower finials.

Choose your quilted border so that it complements the main design of your quilt. Select some of the same motifs and build a border out of flowers, fans, stars or feathers or incorporate a wineglass shape or spiral pattern to match a background texture. You can make an irregular border pattern, such as a waving cable or feather design, fit into a regular shape such as a rectangle or circle by filling in the background with one of the traditional textures like checks or diagonal lines.

Cathedral Window

Crescent and Heart

Feather and Wave intertwined

Fan

Crescent variation

Interlocked Diamonds

This quilted border pattern echoes the wavy binding

Plait

Cable

Plait variation

Plait corner

Intertwined Feathers

Feather variation

Wave variation

Heart and Flower

Spirals

Background textures

Background textures are used to set off the medallions and borders of quilted designs. Originally these were functional; background textures were added to keep the wadding in position and prevent it from bunching. The textures also act as a visual contrast to the main motifs in the quilt.

Choose a pattern in keeping with the style and mood of your main motifs. For instance, if you have a large traditional flower medallion in the centre of your quilt, a subtle chessboard texture or regular diagonal lines will look better than modern asymmetrical zigzags. Wineglass, clamshell, rainbow and spiral designs can easily be marked onto fabric with a circular template if you position it carefully. This is quicker than enlarging a pattern and then tracing it on.

Clamshells

Wineglass

Rainbows

Tartan

Drapes

Diagonal lines

Diagonal lines variation

Diagonal lines variation

Diagonal lines variation

Diagonal lines with Chess-board

Chess-board

Chess-board variation

Zigzag variation

Diamonds

Diamond variation

Spirals

Binding and finishing patterns

The binding of your quilt deserves careful planning. Many complex quilts look best with a relatively plain binding. Bias binding (see page 60) can be used to round off corners or edge a scalloped shape; but binding, bias or straight, doesn't have to be plain. For more visual interest, you can bind a quilt with a patterned fabric from the piecing or make your own strip-pieced binding with straight strips (even or uneven), diamonds or randomly pieced fabrics from the main body of the quilt.

If your project is made from a coarse-weave fabric, fringe the edges, then leave the fringe or cut it into chevrons or scallops or knot it. For delicate items like baby quilts, make a pretty frill. Finish off fine edges with shaped borders made from two layers of fabric seamed in the normal way or edged with hand or machine cutwork in scallops, waves or chevrons.

Curved binding

Straight binding with patterned fabric

Strip-pieced variation

Strip-pieced variation

Scalloped edges

Random pieced binding

Fringed edging

Lace variation

Fringe variation

Lace edging

Knotted edging

Shaped binding

Plain ruffle

Cut-in diamonds

Double ruffles

Shaped variation

Wholecloth motifs

Many of the medallion designs, or wholecloth motifs, shown here are traditional patterns. These, and others, can be combined in an infinite number of patterns and arrangements to fit quilting projects of any size and shape. If you are making a large item, such as a bed quilt or wallhanging, you might want to add a quilted border design (see page 152) or a background texture (see page 154) to set off the main medallions, but the designs are also effective on their own.

Flowers are very common medallion motifs. As these examples show, the petals may be straight, feathered, overlapping, pointed or divided and similar variations can be used on shell and fan shapes. Feathers are also common in quilting designs and you can find or draw a feather design to fit virtually any shape. Emphasize the outline of your medallion with a double row of stitching around the main lines or by echo quilting just outside the edge of the design. Some motifs fit into right angles and are often used as corner designs on a rectangular quilt.

Flower with overlapping petals

Star with echo quilting

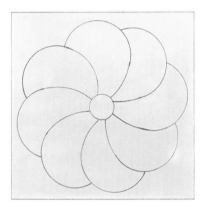

Flower variation

Wholecloth quilt with feather motifs

Feather

Feather in heart shape

Flower with double stitching line

Ring circles

Feather circle

Corner feather

Flower variation

Flower and feather design

Feather circle variation

Amish patterns

Amish quilts are known for their bold use of colour and you can give your Amish project extra authenticity by using a traditional design.

Many Amish quilts are built up from a single block set on point, often an elaborately quilted diamond surrounded by a series of coloured and black borders, each stitched with its own intricate quilting design. Bars and split bars in vivid colours are favourites, again usually surrounded with single or multiple borders. Many Amish borders use a dark strip at the edge with a light square at the corner, or vice versa; the **Garden Maze** *design shown here is also popular. Amish block designs include the* **Double T, Bear's Paw, Pinwheel, Crown of Thorns, Basket** *and* **Tree of Life. Friendship Star** *blocks form a pattern of interlocking stars when joined.* **Trip Around The World** *is a simple design which can be pieced in strips, then cut and reassembled into a stunning quilt top.*

Friendship Star or Batchelor's Puzzle

Water Wheel

Water Wheel variation

Crown of Thorns

Trip Around The World

Double T

Bear's Paw

Garden Maze

Basket

Basket variation

Tree of Life

Typical Amish quilt

English patchwork patterns

Because English patchwork is pieced over paper and doesn't require straight machine seams, any mosaic pattern can be used; try and avoid inside angles (Vs) as they make the piecing considerably more difficult. Draw or trace the shapes very accurately, then use them as templates for cutting fabric and papers. Beautiful designs can be built up using simple squares.

To make the **Clamshell** *design, the outside curves of the fabric shapes are tacked over the papers as usual, then pinned or tacked in rows. The rows are appliquéd on top of each other, with the curved tops of one row concealing the raw edges of the row beneath.*

Tumbling Blocks

Mosaics

Mosaics variation

Triangles

Tumbling Blocks pattern

Octagons

Dark and light

Garden Path

Split hexagons

Clamshells

Diamonds

Diamond variation

Two-tone Diamonds

3-D Diamonds

Multicoloured Diamonds

Sashiko patterns

Most Sashiko patterns are basic geometric shapes built into simple or complex repeat patterns. On quilted kimonos, Japanese designers often used many different patterns in asymmetric shapes (as we did for the evening bag on page 118). Some of these patterns are very straightforward and can be stitched using long straight or curving lines of stitching; others are more complex and have numerous corners or angles, but once you have marked your fabric clearly, the designs are all easy to stitch. If you use several patterns on a project, choose a variety of curves and straight lines, squares, circles and triangles, zigzags and wavy lines.

Curved lines

Interlocking lines

Squares and corners

Interlocking shapes

Sashiko jacket quilted with several different patterns

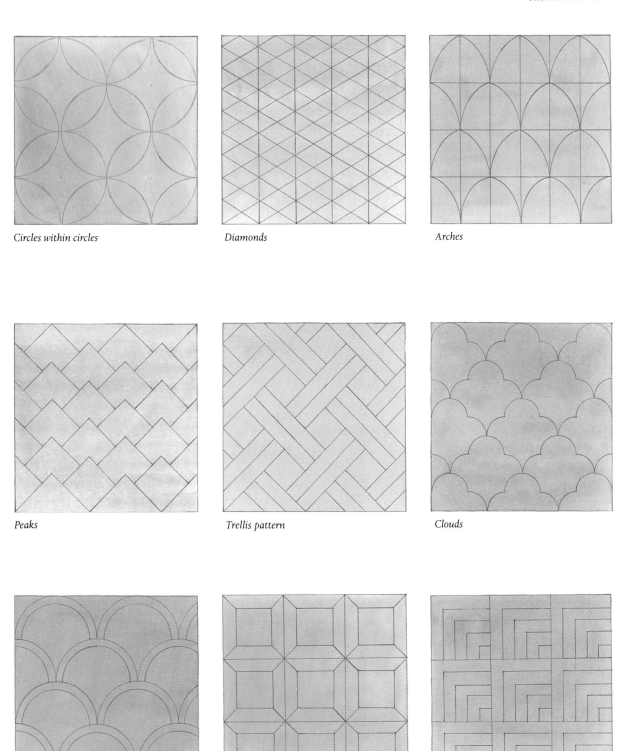

Circles within circles

Diamonds

Arches

Peaks

Trellis pattern

Clouds

Clamshells

Crosses and Squares

Corners

Every quilter dreams of browsing through the attic and discovering an immaculately stitched and perfectly preserved quilt. But the days of magical finds are generally over; most people are aware of the intrinsic value of such beautiful pieces and have rescued them from family storage to use or sell. The most likely way to acquire an old quilt today is to buy it.

Quilts in good condition command high

Restoring and caring for quilts

QUILT CARE

prices, especially if they are detailed. Before you begin any restoration efforts, remember that like any valuable antique, your quilt will depreciate in value if you alter it in any significant way, so you need to decide whether you have bought it as an investment or for your own use or pleasure. If you have bought it as an investment, it will be fine to clean it as long as you don't damage it in any way. If you plan to use it, you may want to restore it by repairing or even replacing damaged sections.

Cleaning old quilts is a very delicate matter; the cleaning process may damage them irreparably. The fabrics may not be colourfast or may not have been pre-shrunk. The wadding may not be washable and, in any case, anything but the most gentle handwashing is likely to damage old fabrics. Always test any soap or cleaning substance on a tiny, unnoticeable area of the quilt in case of disasters. Use cold water, as this is less likely to make fabric colours run; always use the minimum amount of water possible. If you want to display the quilt, getting rid of the worst stains might improve its appearance.

If the fabrics are in good condition, you may want to try dry cleaning, though the quilt may not be robust enough to withstand it. If you know what fibres were used in the fabric and wadding, the dry cleaner will be able to advise you better. If you aren't bothered about keeping the quilt exactly as it was, you can gently unpick a small area to check the

wadding and see if an inner backing fabric was used.

If you want to restore a quilt, you may have to replace worn fabrics or stitching. If a seam has come apart, try to repair it with a ladder stitch so you can work from the right side but still produce an invisible join. If you have to replace pieces of fabric because they have worn through or have been damaged by moths or mould, try to find a fabric as much in keeping with the original as possible. Carefully cut the seams of the damaged pieces of fabric to separate them from the rest of the quilt and use them as templates for cutting new pieces. Stitch as many of the seams as you can in the conventional way, then use ladder stitch to insert the new sections, requilting if necessary.

Old wadding tends to flatten and bunch up. You may be able to fluff it up a little by holding a steam iron just a couple of centimetres away from the quilt surface so the steam can penetrate the quilt. Be careful not to scorch the fabric. If the wadding has bunched up beyond remedy but the pieced quilt top is still in good condition, you might consider removing the backing fabric and requilting the quilt over new wadding. If parts of the quilt are beyond redemption and the thought of cutting up an old quilt doesn't horrify you, cut out a good section and use it as a baby quilt, a cushion cover, to decorate a piece of clothing or mount it as a picture.

Quilts can become damaged very easily if not handled with care. Edging is particularly vulnerable to fraying through general wear and tear.

There are many ways of displaying quilts. Attach fabric casing or tape loops (see right and middle) to the back of the quilt along one edge. The quilt can now be hung from a rod.

Sew Velcro strips (far right) to fabric and attach the fabric to the back of the quilt. Sew the matching Velcro strips to a fabric-covered frame or other surface. The quilt can now be stretched and hung using the Velcro fastenings.

Although many gallery and museum quilts are constantly on display, protective measures are taken to ensure they don't fade or gather dirt. When displaying a quilt at home, avoid strong light and excessive moisture and try to keep it in a constant temperature.

Sew Velcro strips (right) to fabric and attach the fabric to the back of the quilt. Sew the Velcro loops to a fabric-covered frame or other surface. The quilt can now be stretched and hung using the Velcro fastenings.

Glossary

ALBUM QUILT
A quilt made up of different appliqué blocks, sometimes all the same but often with different designs in each block; also called a Baltimore quilt.

AMISH QUILTING
A distinctive style of quilting of the Amish, a religious group known for their simple lifestyle.

APPLIQUÉ
A decorative technique which involves stitching one piece of fabric on top of another.

BACKING FABRIC
A piece of fabric, often plain, used to back a quilt or other item.

BACK STITCH
An embroidery stitch used to create a firm line or outline.

BIAS BINDING
A narrow strip of fabric, cut diagonally across the grain, used for binding seams and edges, especially curves.

BINDING
The edging of a quilt which covers and holds all raw edges. Bindings may be plain or decorative.

BLOCK
A small section of patchwork, usually square; most quilts are made from a number of pieced blocks joined together.

BODKIN
A large needle with a large eye used for pulling cord, thick yarn, elastic, etc., through a casing or channel.

BORDER
A decorative pattern which runs around the edges of a quilt top. Borders may be straight, curved, flowing, swagged and may be pieced or quilted or both.

BRODERIE ANGLAISE
An embroidered lace, white eyelet on white cotton, available as fabric or edging.

BRODERIE PERSE
An appliqué technique using motifs cut from printed fabric.

CALICO
Inexpensive plain weave cotton fabric often used as a backing fabric or a layer under wadding.

CASING
A channel of fabric or tape stitched to the back of a quilt through which a rod is inserted.

CATHEDRAL WINDOW PATCHWORK
Patchwork which involves folding squares of fabric into 'frames'; the 'windows' are filled with contrasting fabric.

CHARM QUILT
A pieced quilt in which every piece is the same shape, but cut from a different fabric.

CORDED QUILTING
Another name for Italian quilting.

CRAZY QUILT
Quilt made from random sizes and shapes of fancy fabrics such as velvets and silks; the patchwork is embellished with ornate embroidery along seam lines.

CUTTING MAT
A vinyl mat used under a rotary cutter.

DRESSMAKER'S CARBON PAPER
Coloured carbon paper used for transferring designs or patterns on to fabric.

ECHO QUILTING
Concentric lines of quilting stitches worked around an outline at regular intervals.

ENGLISH PATCHWORK
A patchwork technique in which the fabric patches are tacked over paper templates, then joined before the templates are removed.

FABRIC PAINT
Craft paint formulated for use on fabric; may be specific to particular fibres such as silk. Many fabric paints require heat to be set permanently.

FADING-INK PEN
A pen used for marking quilting patterns on fabric; ink fades naturally in light over time.

FOLDED PATCHWORK
Pieced work made from fabric folded into points; typically assembled in star patterns.

FOUR-PATCH BLOCK
A patchwork design made from four rectangular pieces; individual squares can be pieced designs as well.

FRAME
A device used for stretching fabric flat. Quilting frames may be fairly small or large enough to hold an entire quilt top.

FRILL
A gathered edging of fabric or lace.

GRAIN
The straight warp or weft of a fabric. The direction of the grain is very important when cutting patchwork pieces or pattern designs.

GRAPH PAPER
Paper marked into small squares and used for drawing templates and patterns; also used to reduce and enlarge designs.

HEM
A finished edge, usually made by folding a raw edge over twice and stitching it down.

HOOP
A circular or oval quilting frame.

ITALIAN QUILTING
A decorative method of threading cord or wool through channels stitched onto a double layer of fabric.

KAPA LAU
Hawaiian appliqué quilting; large, complex designs are appliquéd onto a background fabric and enhanced with echo quilting.

LADDER STITCH
Used for making an invisible seam from the right side.

LIGHT BOX

A box with light inside and opaque glass on top; used in quilting for tracing patterns on to fabric or paper.

MEDALLION QUILT

A quilt design featuring one large central pattern or motif.

METALLICS

Fabrics or threads which have a metallic appearance.

MITRED CORNERS

Corners of a binding which are joined with a diagonal (45°) seam rather than with a straight one.

NINE-PATCH BLOCK

A square block design made from nine square patches, three across and three down. Individual squares may be pieced designs in themselves.

ON POINT

Mounting a square block at an angle in a quilt top so that it appears as a diamond.

PATCHWORK

Joining one or more fabric shapes to make a pattern.

PIECING

Another name for patchwork.

PRICK AND POUNCE

Transferring designs to fabric by making holes along the main lines of the paper patterns and dusting chalk or other powder through the holes on to the fabric.

QUILTER'S QUARTER

A rectangular plastic rod used for adding 5 mm (¼ in) seam allowances to straight edges of fabrics or templates.

QUILTING

Stitching a decorative pattern through three layers, usually quilt top, wadding and backing.

QUILTING BEE

A group of people working together on the same quilt.

QUILTING IN THE DITCH

Quilting in which the stitching lines run next to the seam lines.

QUILTING NEEDLE

A long, strong needle helpful for making tiny quilting stitches.

QUILTING THREAD

A strong thread, often waxed, made specifically for quilting; available in many colours.

ROLLER FRAME

A large frame to hold a whole quilt; most of the quilt is scrolled onto the end rollers, leaving one section exposed for quilting.

ROTARY CUTTER

A circular blade used for cutting several layers of fabric simultaneously.

RUNNING STITCH

A straight stitch, used for most hand quilting.

SATIN STITCH

A stitch with a very short width; each stitch touches the next.

SASHIKO

A Japanese style of quilting, worked with long stitches in repetitive, often geometric, patterns.

SASHING

Strips of fabric used to separate blocks on a quilt top.

SILVERPOINT

Pencil-shaped metal implement used for marking quilting designs on to fabric.

SOMERSET PATCHWORK

A type of folded patchwork.

STAINED GLASS PATCHWORK

Patchwork method where the seams between fabrics are covered with bias strips to simulate 'leading'.

STRAIGHT BINDING

A method of binding the edges of a quilt with straight pieces of fabric cut exactly along the grain.

STRAIGHT STITCH

The standard sewing stitch; has length, but no width.

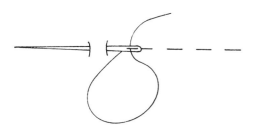

STUFFING

Soft fibres used for filling the pockets in trapunto quilting.

TACKING

A long, running stitch used to hold fabrics in place temporarily.

TEMPLATE

An accurate, full-size design used as a tracing and cutting guide; may be made from plastic, metal, paper or card.

TEMPLATE PLASTIC

A transparent or translucent plastic sheet ideal for making templates.

TONE

The shade of a particular colour.

TRAPUNTO

A quilting technique which adds extra stuffing to small pockets stitched into a double layer of fabric.

VALUE

The lightness or darkness of a colour.

VELCRO

A fastening material in which one layer of small plastic hooks adheres to another layer of small loops.

WADDING

A layer of padding for quilted work made of natural or synthetic fibres and available in several thicknesses.

WALKING FOOT

A sewing machine foot to enable top and bottom fabric layers to feed at same speed.

WATER-SOLUBLE INK PEN

A pen used for marking quilting patterns on fabric; ink fades when sponged with water.

WHOLECLOTH QUILTING

A quilting method where the top layer is a single large piece of fabric; the design is made with quilting stitches rather than patchwork.

ZIGZAG

A basic machine sewing back-and-forth stitch; has width as well as length.

Index

Page references in *italics* refer to pictures.

Acknowledgments

The publishers would like to acknowledge and thank the following for their help in the production of this book, especially the quilters whose work is featured.

page 1	Jenny Rees
page 2/3	Janice Gunner
page 4/5	Janine Whiteson
page 8/9	Jenny Rees
page 10/11	Janice Gunner
page 12/13	BEAMISH, The North of Engand Open Air Museum, County Durham
page 14/15	Crane Gallery, London
page 16/17	Crane Gallery, London
page 19	Alison Findlay/National Patchwork Championships
page 21	Shelburne Museum, Shelburne, Vermont
(top)	Shipley Art Gallery, Tyne and Wear Museums
(bottom)	Marilyn Garrow
page 22/23	Janine Whiteson
page 24/25	Judith Hammersla
page 34 (top)	Rose Hunneyball/National Patchwork Championships
(bottom)	Janice Gunner
page 38/39 (left)	Rosalie Rakow/National Patchwork Championships
(right)	Louise Bell
page 40	templates Chattels, London
page 46	Crane Gallery, London
page 50	Crane Gallery, London
page 57	Jenny Rees
page 57	Janice Gunner
page 60	Crane Gallery, London
page 62/63	Gail Lawther
page 100/101	Jenny Rees
page 102	Gail Lawther
page 104	Gail Lawther
page 105	Gail Lawther
page 106	Gail Lawther

Special thanks to the Quilt Room, 20 West Street, Dorking, Surrey RH4 1BL (mail order available), whose equipment is featured throughout this book.

page 108	Gail Lawther
page 110	Gail Lawther
page 112	Angela Besley
page 114	Gail Lawther
page 116	Gail Lawther
page 118	Margaret Blakeley
page 122/123	Jenny Rees
page 124 (top)	Jenny Rees
(bottom)	Shelburne Museum, Shelburne, Vermont
page 125 (top)	Shelburne Museum, Shelburne, Vermont
(bottom left)	Crane Gallery, London
(botton right)	Deirdre Amsden
page 126	Crane Gallery, London
page 128	Shelburne Museum, Shelburne, Vermont
page 132	Crane Gallery, London
page 134	Crane Gallery, London
page 136	Gill Turley
page 138	Pamela Cross
page 140	Crane Gallery, London
page 144	Jenny Rees
page 152	Shelburne Museum, Shelburne, Vermont
page 158	BEAMISH, The North of England Open Air Museum, County Durham
page 160	Shelburne Museum, Shelburne, Vermont
page 164	Sashiko jacket, Margaret Blakeley
page 168	Shelburne Museum, Shelburne, Vermont
page 169	Shelburne Museum, Shelburne, Vermont
page 171	Crane Gallery, London.